"Wexler gives us a uniqu
depressed men, men whos
whose coping skills may r
descriptions of desperately
be particularly enlightenir
of men who turn mean o
Depressed or What? will sa

—Frank S. Pittmar
Sons, and the S

"Is He Depressed or Wh
relationship with a depr
yet grounded in commo
specific tools and strate
struggling with depressi

—Rosalind Wisema

is he depressed or what?

What to Do When the Man You Love Is Irritable, Moody, and Withdrawn

DAVID B. WEXLER, PH.D.

New Harbinger Publications, Inc.

Distributed in Canada by Raincoast Books

Copyright © 2005 by David B. Wexler
New Harbinger Publications, Inc.
5674 Shattuck Avenue
Oakland, CA 94609

Cover design by Amy Shoup; Text design by Tracy Marie Carlson; Acquired by Melissa Kirk; Edited by Carole Honeychurch

---

Library of Congress Cataloging-in-Publication Data
Wexler, David B.
  Is he depressed or what? : what to do when the man you love is irritable, moody, and withdrawn / David B. Wexler.
       p. cm.
  Includes bibliographical references.
  ISBN 1-57224-424-0 (pbk.)
  1. Depression in men. 2. Depression, Mental—Patients—Family relationships. I. Title.
  RC537.W42 2006
  616.85'270081—dc22

                                                2005029511

New Harbinger Publications' Web site address: www.newharbinger.com

07   06   05
10   9   8   7   6   5   4   3   2   1

First printing

To my parents, Sydney and Cynthia

Contents

Acknowledgments

Many thanks to Melissa Kirk of New Harbinger Publications, who first approached me with this notion of a book for women who were trying to deal with a depressed man in their life. She, and the editors who helped shape this work (Carole Honeychurch, Kayla Sussell, and Heather Mitchener), all shared and respected my vision of the proper tone for this book: compassionate toward men and empowering toward women. It has been a pleasure to work with this team. Thanks also to Shelley Cline for her terrific work assembling the Resources section to help you get what you need.

I would also like to thank my wife's sisters, Chris Kidd, Janice Horowitz, and Regina Brunig, who have always been as excited and sometimes more excited than I have been about the ideas in this book and my other books. Their enthusiasm and wisdom in shaping the ideas here have been invaluable. And, always, my deep appreciation to the most important people: my daughter, Juliana, my son, Joe, and my wife, Connie. They put up with all my trips to Starbucks with my laptop and give meaning to everything I do.

Without the men and women whom I have worked with over the years, this book would have been nothing but an academic exercise. Thanks to all of you, on both sides of this fence, for allowing me to know you, learn from you, and borrow some of your stories to pass on to others. You know who you are.

And one more special thanks to my parents, Sydney and Cynthia, who didn't teach me much about irritable, moody, or withdrawn men—but taught me plenty.

Introduction

Male depression was a well-kept secret until the publication of Terrence Real's *I Don't Want To Talk About It: Overcoming the Secret Legacy of Male Depression* (1997), William Pollack's *Real Boys* (1998b), and Jed Diamond's *Male Menopause* (1997). Many national education campaigns to highlight the hidden signs of male depression have sprouted in the past few years. The National Institute of Mental Health (NIMH) began an outreach campaign to reduce the stigma of men seeking help for depression, citing the experiences of a firefighter, police officer, and diving champion who had all been treated for the condition (NIMH 2004).

There have since been several new books about male depression, but none for you—the partners of depressed men—and certainly none that rely on the newest models of how depression shows up in men.

It might make sense to drop the use of the word "depression" here, because if you're looking for obvious signs and symptoms of depression that we all recognize, you might miss the cluster of signs and symptoms that are particularly male. Male depression often shows itself differently than female depression. Men who appear active and "successful" often mask depression with workaholism, substance abuse, withdrawal from intimate relationships, and defensive (and sometimes aggressive) interpersonal behavior. Depressed men are more likely to talk about physical symptoms of depression such as headaches, insomnia, and stomach upset, rather than emotional symptoms. Furthermore, depressed men are more likely to attempt—and succeed at—suicide. Often, the man's romantic partner is the one who notices the depression before he or his doctor does. And even then it may look like something else.

I have often reflected back about the period of my life in my thirties when I was flat on my back with sciatica pain from a protruded disk. My wife had to cook my meals, help me up to go to the bathroom, and bring me whatever I had forgotten to ask her for the first time. And I was often in a bad mood, snapping at her and getting irritable when she didn't take care of things just the way I wanted her to. The combination of being in chronic pain and feeling depressed, discouraged, and inadequate from needing so much help turned my normally sunny personality solid grey with intermittent storminess. I couldn't see how I was affecting my wife or what she at least occasionally needed from me. I only had room to take care of one person at a time.

The worst feature of all, the often overlooked signal of an underlying male depression, was the blame. I felt bad, didn't like it, and didn't know what to call it. So I looked around and found someone whose fault it might have been. Hers.

Identifying and talking about the classic feelings associated with depression—feeling helpless, unmotivated, unsuccessful, unlovable—run profoundly counter to the classic masculine self-identity. This book will help you recognize the types of obstacles that may be getting in the way for the man in your life and help you offer what you can to help him free himself from these obstacles.

This book is about depressed men and helping you, as a partner of such a man, do the best for him, for yourself, and for the relationship. But the title of this book may make you nervous, because you may worry about your partner's reaction to being identified by you as a depressed man. Language is very important to people and the label of depression is especially shaming to many men.

You may not want to label him as depressed because his defensiveness may end the conversation. Remember that one of the deepest fears for many men is becoming too "feminine," and even acknowledging a simple label like "depressed" may conjure up an unbearable and unacceptable retreat into the world of the feminine. I repeat: language is very important. Many men can admit to feeling "stressed" or "tired" in a heartbeat, but wouldn't be caught dead describing themselves as "depressed." Lots of men might consider consulting their physician for something to help with stress but would never look for a therapist to work on their depression.

But no matter what you learn to label it for yourself, when it comes to talking to men about the themes of this book, it is time to get very creative about what you say and when you say it. Under these circumstances, and in the spirit of reaching your most important audience member, it's okay to not call it by its real name, as long as you call it *something* and the issues start getting addressed.

WHAT TO EXPECT

The first section of this book will help you recognize the many faces of male depression that are often disguised as something else and help your partner get properly diagnosed. Next, you will learn how to effectively communicate with a depressed man and how to deal with relationship issues that may be intensified by the depression. You will also learn about how to cope with side effects such as insomnia and sexual dysfunction and how to (or whether to) communicate with family and friends about your partner's depression.

And, most importantly, the final chapters of this book will help you take care of yourself emotionally, psychologically, and behaviorally. It will help you learn how to be a loving and supportive partner without becoming an enabler or losing yourself in the process. And it will also help you make the best possible decisions about whether the burdens of your partner's depressive patterns are more than you can handle.

Throughout this book are exercises designed to help you to make sense of what you are observing in your partner and to help you respond with the greatest likelihood of success. I recommend that you designate a specific notebook or journal in which to complete the different exercises as you go along.

There's a chance that this book may not help you. Learning about male depression might not make much of a difference in dealing with your partner. Even if you try a lot of the strategies and interventions, it's possible that they won't have that much of an impact. The man in your life may read this book, too, or learn from what you have learned, and he still may not recover or get much of a break in the storm clouds of his mood. So it goes with depression.

However, most of you will find just the opposite. The more you know about how male depression really works and what to do about it, the more likely that this information—combined with all the thousands of things you already know and do well—will make a difference. And the new perspectives on what your role realistically can be and what your truest and most honorable options are should free you up so you can be the best partner you can be and make the best possible choices you can make.

CHAPTER 1

Typical Depression:
The Guy Who
Looks Depressed

Some of you know what it's like to be in a relationship with a man like Shawn. He has trouble getting out of bed in the morning. He has lost a job, or maybe he is performing at a mediocre level at his current job. He seems like a lost soul. Not very many areas of his life turn Shawn on—not food or friends, not sex or sports, not work or kids. He worries a lot and doubts his own decisions. He knows there is something wrong with him but doesn't quite know what to call it. And when you ask him, for the thousandth time, "What's wrong?" his face turns a shade darker, he curls up in his shell, and shrugs his shoulders. He tells you, "I'm just tired, I guess." This depression comes out only in small ways, because he's trying to show his best self. But you can tell he feels bad about himself and often sorry for himself.

It's hard to be mad at Shawn, because he's a nice guy. He seems so burdened that you feel for him and would like to lift his spirits. On the other hand, sometimes you become frustrated with him, and you just want to shake him out of it. His troubles may feel like a burden to you—but you feel guilty acknowledging this to yourself or others.

This is called *typical depression,* or *overt depression.* Even though Shawn may be reluctant to seek help or to label his moods and feelings with the "D" word, his version of depression is not significantly different from typical signs and symptoms of depression in women. It is pretty obvious to almost anyone that something is wrong, and you don't have to be a trained clinician to think of labeling this as depression.

Some of you also know what it's like to be in a relationship with a man like Mike. Nothing about Mike is quiet or withdrawn. He can be very boisterous and energetic. He works ridiculously long hours and is very successful in his field—except that he sometimes blows up and ruins business relationships or loses a job. He drinks to excess and sometimes snorts coke. Mike's on his third marriage. Every woman he has ever been with has been drawn to his exciting personality, but has eventually been driven away by his moodiness and self-centered behavior. More and more, he seems to seek out reckless and risk-taking behavior, which sometimes backfires on him. He may be having affairs or seeking the stimulation of other women who recharge his batteries. He has periods of restlessness and unhappiness, which he usually blames on his partner or his kids. He identifies himself as a "man's man" and overreacts when he feels as if he has been (or is perceived to have been) unsuccessful or ineffective.

Every once in a while Mike breaks down and you see how much he is hurting inside. He often feels and acts remorseful after he acts badly with you or the kids.

Sometimes it's hard to feel much compassion for Mike, because he doesn't treat you well enough often enough. It's confusing: he blames you when he is feeling moody or unhappy, and you probably know it's because he has very little capacity to tolerate any negative feelings, which feel profoundly unmasculine to him. But Mike can also be exciting, dynamic, and sexy, and he is often a wonderful dad who loves his kids passionately. A lot of the time you feel as if you are failing him or falling short. You can usually tell that there is a hurt boy and a better man inside that don't often show themselves. This is called *male-type depression* (also known as *male depressive disorder* or *covert depression*).

Both Shawn and Mike are depressed. Shawn is depressed in the ways that almost everyone understands, and the symptoms of this kind of depression transcend gender. But Mike suffers from a particularly male kind of depression that we are only recently beginning to recognize and make sense out of.

You and your partner need to recognize both varieties of depression.

Researchers estimate that between three and four million men in the United States suffer from some sort of a depressive disorder every year (National Institute of Mental Health 2002). Although there are plenty of exceptions, men are more willing to acknowledge fatigue, irritability, loss of interest in work or hobbies, and sleep disturbances rather than feelings of sadness, worthlessness, and excessive guilt. The masking of depression through denial, minimization, escapist and addictive behaviors, defensiveness, blaming, and aggression appears much more frequently in men, while the presence of anxiety is much more prevalent for women.

Recent studies (Potts, Burnam, and Wells 1991) have highlighted the profound underdiagnosis of depression in men. When they compared how many men in a given group were diagnosed with depression to the results when these same men completed a specific standard depression questionnaire, they found that 65 percent of these men's verified depressions went undetected and undiagnosed. In other words, almost two-thirds of men who were actively suffering from a depression had their illness undetected and untreated.

WHAT TYPICAL DEPRESSION LOOKS LIKE

First, let's look at more typical signs of depression. Much of this information looks the same for men as for women, but there are certain patterns that especially plague men. In chapter 2, we will look at the not-so-obvious patterns of depression in men and the ways that men's acculturation and neurochemistry have trained them to handle it.

When the cloud of depression hovers over your partner's life, even the basics like eating, sleeping, and paying attention no longer operate on "automatic pilot," and they often become problems. A man locked in the grip of depression struggles to meet even the most minimal demands on his resources. Getting through the day tends to use up all of his energy, making it difficult to feel desire or joy. This is often worsened because he may have trouble remembering that he actually once had those feelings or believing he might have any chance of experiencing them in the future.

Depression affects the man's self-concept and the way he thinks about things. A true depressive disorder is not the same as a passing blue mood. It is not a sign of personal weakness or a condition that can be willed or wished away. People with a depressive illness cannot merely pull themselves together and get better.

The Negative Triad of Self-Talk

Researcher Aaron Beck (1976) detailed in his original formulations the crucial role of cognitions, or *self-talk*, in determining how we feel. In other words, what we think about our experiences directly affects how we feel about them. Self-talk is essential in generating, maintaining, and potentially relieving depression, and manifests itself in what Beck called the "negative triad":

1. Negative views of the self

2. Negative views of others

3. Negative views of the future

Self-talk represents the story that people tell themselves about the world around them. We are constantly spinning stories to put events, other people, and ourselves into perspective. Our brains are hardwired to make sense of things, but this does not guarantee that we're telling ourselves the right story, only that we insist on telling ourselves at least some kind of story. Worst of all is that the times when a depressed person desperately needs to have all his best resources available to him—including the most positive, hopeful, or charitable story—are the times when these are the most inaccessible. A man who is withdrawing from his kids because he feels so ineffective is desperately in need of self-talk that reminds himself of his strengths and lovability. And he desperately needs to maintain a fundamental optimism about his capacity to learn something from what he is going through and that he can do it better in the future.

Unfortunately, faced with these circumstances, he is more likely to retreat into pessimism, defeatism, and blame:

"I'll never be able to pull this off."

"I can't seem to be what my wife wants me to be."

"I don't think I'm cut out for this 'fatherhood' (or 'relationship') thing."

"There must be something wrong with *them*."

Or, more tragically, as more than one of my male clients have told me, "It seems like I mess up everyone who I've ever become close to."

My client Andrea described the conversations with her husband when he was tailspinning:

He would describe the problems in our marriage with words like "nightmare" or "catastrophe" or "disaster." When he was in a better mood, he knew these descriptions were way over the top, and that more appropriate words would be "sometimes frustrating" or "up and down" or "lots of good times mixed in with problems that we're both working on." But when he is in one of his moods he forgets it all, and it all looks dark. And he acts dark.

A snapshot of the self-talk of the depressed man will show you a pattern of frequent, long-lasting, and intense negative thought patterns. Neutral situations generate negative spin. Disappointing events generate a catastrophic spin. And the spin lasts longer than for the nondepressed. A depressed man is also more likely to turn ordinary negative experiences, which are specific, external, and temporary, into tragic stories that are global, internal, and permanent.

Depression and Pessimism

Martin Seligman (2004) is the leading researcher on optimistic thinking styles and *positive psychology*, which he defines as concentrating on well-being and satisfaction, flow and joy, sensual pleasures and happiness. It emphasizes constructive beliefs about the future: optimism, hope, and faith. According to Seligman (1998), the three crucial dimensions of a person's self-explanatory style are *permanence, pervasiveness,* and *personalization.* In other words, the defining characteristic of pessimists is that they tend to believe bad events will last a long time, will undermine everything they do, and are their own fault. Optimists, despite being exposed to the same circumstances and often being dealt the same crummy hands, think about negative events very differently. They see frustrations as temporary setbacks and believe that the causes are specific to the incident. When failure or frustration hits, optimists are more likely to identify the source as circumstances, bad luck, or because of other people. Frustrations are only temporary setbacks. Optimists tend to perceive these situations as challenges and to use them to generate solutions and action plans.

Self-Efficacy

Albert Bandura's perspectives on how personal beliefs or personal narratives affect one's sense of well-being and govern the likelihood of positive activity are illustrated by his research on *self-efficacy.* Self-efficacy reflects the belief that we have the capacity to be effective or efficacious. Bandura's (1997) most fundamental statement about the role of self-efficacy beliefs in human functioning points out that people's level of motivation, emotional states, and actions are based more on what they believe than on what is objectively true. These self-efficacy perceptions help determine what individuals actually do with the knowledge and skills they have.

This dynamic helps explain why people's behaviors are sometimes jarringly incongruent with their actual capabilities and why their behavior may differ widely even when they have similar knowledge and skills. For example, many talented men suffer frequent (and sometimes debilitating) bouts of self-doubt about capabilities they clearly possess, just as many other men are confident about what they can accomplish despite possessing a modest repertoire of skills. Belief and reality are seldom perfectly matched, and people are guided by their beliefs when they engage the world. In other words, what he thinks about who he is and what he is capable of is as good or sometimes even a better predictor of future performance than some absolute measure of pure skill or capacity. (Of course, this concept shouldn't be taken to the point of ridiculousness: no amount of confidence or self-appreciation can produce success when requisite skills and knowledge are absent).

For the depressed man, negative thoughts occur easily, without intention, and require only minimal amounts of cognitive capacity. Conversely, positive thinking requires more intention and effort. The darker perspective becomes habitual and feels normal. Challenging these patterns seems foreign and unnatural.

As many of you know, sometimes the man who has retreated into a darker perspective about himself, others, and his future just withdraws and shuts down in discouragement. And other men (or the same man at another time), in a desperate attempt to ward off these bad feelings and shameful stories, become nasty, blaming, and aggressive. It's still depression at the core, just expressed differently. Shawn and Mike—or sometimes a combination of the two.

As your partner looks at himself or the world around him, there may even be evidence to confirm the darker and more pessimistic story that he's telling himself. There is almost always evidence when you are looking for it. In almost all situations, however, there is also evidence to support a more positive spin. It's just that, at the times when it would be most valuable for him to tell himself the positive story, he can't hear it. Or else he can hear it, but he believes it only applies to someone else.

Rumination

One of the self-talk patterns that can be so paralyzing in the midst of depression is *rumination,* or going over and over negative thoughts. Seligman (1998) reports that one of the main determinants of whether a depressed mood will persist or lift is the degree to which people ruminate. It is difficult enough to actually be depressed or anxious, but worrying about when these states will take over or what's causing them creates a double wallop of psychic pain and draining of psychic energy. Even worse is when the depressed man blames himself for feeling this way, so that he feels bad and then feels bad about feeling bad.

Research studies (Nolen-Hoeksema 1993) have identified several rumination patterns like the following that plague depressed men. A depressed man may manifest the following behaviors:

- isolate himself and then spend a lot of time thinking about how terrible he feels;

- worry that his partner will reject him because he is depressed;

- dread nighttime because he is worried that he's going to have another sleepless night;

- worry so much about depression that he can't get around to following through on work assignments.

Your partner with more typical, overt depression probably engages in patterns of overanalyzing and ruminating—just as is typical for women—often justifying this pattern by claiming that introspection will help him figure everything out better. Such things are possible. During difficult times, facing difficult challenges, most of us benefit from thinking things over. But, at some point, we reach a point of diminishing returns. The introspection bleeds into rumination, and the potential for analysis that might trigger productive action degenerates into worrying that triggers nothing but more worry and paralysis.

The greater the levels of anxiety accompanying depression, the greater the tendency to ruminate. This pattern of rumination is paralyzing and self-defeating, and there are only two known paths to loosening its vise-grip: *reframing* (developing new narratives) and *distraction* (refocusing or interrupting the negative ruminations). Throughout this book, you will learn more about the effective use of both of these strategies and how you can increase the likelihood of your partner's success with these psychological lifesavers. Both reframing and distraction can also be helpful to you when you are feeling overwhelmed or depressed about your partner's mood.

Anhedonia

Anhedonia is a killer. The roots of this word come from the Greek word *hedone*, meaning pleasure. *Anhedonia* refers to the inability to experience pleasure. It's as if the brain has established little synapse gatekeepers who check ID for possibly pleasurable, satisfying, or rewarding nerve impulses and then won't allow them entrance into the club. Jimmy, a client of mine, put it this way: "I pretty much lost interest in just about everything. I just felt dead inside, like I was going through the motions." It's not only the big sources of pleasure that lose their impact, like sex or getting a major job promotion. It's the little stuff as well. Imagine life without all the little events in a typical day that offer jolts of reward. That's what it's like to be depressed. Drinking a cup of coffee. Hearing something funny on the radio. Watching your daughter get excited about something she's doing. Taking a shower. Reading the newspaper and finding out that your team won last night or that your presidential candidate gained a few points in the polls or that some of your stocks went up in value. Just plopping into bed and feeling the covers around you. The list goes on. Some people are more blessed with these events and, perhaps more importantly, with the capacity to take them in and genuinely benefit from them. But when someone is depressed, these little potential endorphin infusions (bursts of pleasurable neurochemicals) lose their punch. They are just more stuff, grey—like everything else.

Again, at the time when your partner is most desperate for bursts (or even little trickles) of pleasure, his brain and body won't let them in. The nondepressed can get by for a while with fewer pleasurable experiences. But someone who is depressed desperately needs pleasure. Ironically, his depression makes pleasure pretty much unrecognizable. His brain and body screen it out.

When you observe a depressed guy giving up, avoiding things, and appearing to be unmotivated, it's usually because he can't get this mantra out of his brain: "What's the point? It won't make me feel any better anyway."

Even sex, a sure-fire source of pleasure for most guys, gets swallowed in his negative mood. Depression and sexual interest are almost always inversely correlated. When a man who has previously had a lively sexual interest starts to lose it, there are a thousand possible explanations. But one, of course, is depression, and this can best be understood in the context of the anhedonia experience. Hard as it may be to believe to people who enjoy sex, the depressed guy will begin to think of sex as one more of those "what's the point?" experiences. And it can be especially discouraging and depressing to this guy when even sex—the last bastion of guaranteed pleasure—crashes and burns.

The exceptions to this pattern of anhedonically-driven withdrawal from life take place when the man desperately seeks excessive stimulation in an attempt to jump-start the failing pleasure receptors.

You will hear more about stimulation seekers in the next section. For now, just remember that depression, especially depression in men, can and often does show up in forms that appear to be 180 degrees opposite from each other. The overtly depressed man who appears despondent and discouraged is not fundamentally different from the covertly depressed man who overachieves, overdrinks, and overblames (as you will learn in the next chapter). Anhedonia can generate desperate lust for more intense excitement and pleasure just as easily as it can promote a withdrawal from any attempts to have these experiences.

IDENTIFYING YOUR PARTNER'S DEPRESSION

Below is a questionnaire for you to fill out to help you assess whether the man in your life is experiencing typical, or overt, depression. In the right-hand column, score 0 if the item is not a problem, 1 if it's something of a problem, and 2 if it is very noticeable or serious.

EXERCISE: Signs and Symptoms of Overt Depression

AFFECTIVE/EMOTIONAL	Score 0, 1, or 2
1. Does your partner feel sad and miserable most of the time (nearly every day)?	
2. Does he become frightened for no apparent reason? Do his fears seem exaggerated?	
3. Does he experience fits of crying or has he mentioned feeling like crying all the time?	
4. Does he seem restless and agitated?	
5. Is he unusually irritable?	
6. Does he express feelings of emptiness and guilt?	

BEHAVIORAL

7. Has he lost interest in activities he used to enjoy?	6
8. Does he seem apathetic or lethargic? Is it hard for him to get motivated in the morning?	
9. Are his movements, speech, and decision making slower than usual?	
10. Is his performance at work deteriorating?	
11. Has he been purposefully or absentmindedly engaging in risky behavior such as driving through red lights or not wearing a seat belt?	0
12. Have you noticed an increase in his use of alcohol or other drugs?	2

INTERPERSONAL

13. Has he lost interest in sex?	2
14. Has he suddenly become much more dependent and clingy?	0
15. Does he tend to blame you and others more when he is in a bad mood?	
16. When the phone rings, does he tend to ignore it even when he knows it may be a good friend calling?	0
17. Has he been turning down invitations to get together with friends because he thinks his "down" mood will just depress everyone else?	0

COGNITIVE/SELF-TALK

18. Does he seem confused or forgetful? Does he have difficulty making decisions?	
19. Does he express feelings of worthlessness? Does he seem especially discouraged about the future?	
20. Does he complain that everything is going wrong no matter how hard he's trying?	
21. Does he ever make comments like "You'd all be better off if I weren't around"?	

SOMATIC/PHYSICAL	
22. Is he having difficulty sleeping? Or does he sleep for hours on end without actually feeling rested?	
23. Does he seem exhausted most of the time?	
24. Does he complain of persistent physical symptoms with no obvious origin that don't seem to respond to routine treatment?	
25. Has he had noticeable changes in his appetite? Has he lost a significant amount of weight (5 percent of his body weight in a month) without dieting? Or is he suddenly overeating?	
SCORE	

This is not a scientific tool for proper diagnosis, so there is no absolute cutoff established for determining true depression. But it should give you a guideline to either confirm your suspicions or quell them. Any score of 10 or above suggests depression, and anything over 20 should serve as a major red flag. Please remember that this measures only one type of male depression—overt depression. The other kind will be addressed in the next chapter.

TYPES OF TYPICAL DEPRESSION

Some depressions are acute, but they pass. They are normal reactions to stressful, disturbing, or painful human events. Your husband loses his job and withdraws for a few weeks, or suffers the loss of a parent and seems sexually uninterested and unmotivated in general for several months. Or he's just moody for a while with no obvious trigger. These episodes are painful, difficult to live with, and simply depressing, but they are distinctly different from some of the more chronic and debilitating long-standing patterns of a depressive condition or depressive personality. None of these are easy, but some are worse than others and tougher to change.

The Four Major Types of Typical Depression

In the standard diagnostic manual for mental-health disorders (American Psychiatric Association 2000), four main types of depression are identified:

Major depression (or major depressive disorder) is characterized by a combination of symptoms that interferes with the ability to work, study, sleep, eat, and enjoy once-pleasurable activities. A major depressive episode may occur only once, but more commonly, several episodes may occur in a lifetime. Major depression often includes thoughts about suicide or actual suicide attempts. Chronic major depression may require a person to continue treatment indefinitely.

A less severe type of depression, **dysthymia (or dysthymic disorder),** involves long-lasting symptoms that do not seriously disable but keep the person from functioning well or feeling good. It's a technical term for a situation that we observe and live with frequently: mild to moderate depression that goes on for a long time but never quite pushes somebody over the edge to suicide, total despair, or incapacitation. Many people with dysthymia also experience major depressive episodes at some time in their lives.

Another type of depressive illness occurs with **bipolar disorder (or manic-depressive illness)**. Bipolar disorder is characterized by cycling mood changes: severe highs (mania) and lows (depression), often with periods of normal mood in between. Sometimes the mood switches are dramatic and rapid, but usually they are gradual. When in the depressed cycle, an individual can have any or all of the symptoms of depression. When in the manic cycle, the individual may be overactive, overtalkative, and have a great deal of energy. Mania often affects thinking, judgment, and social behavior in ways that cause serious problems and embarrassment. For example, in a manic phase your partner may feel elated, believe himself to be invincible, and concoct grand schemes that might range from unwise business decisions to physical risk-taking to outrageous gambling to reckless, unsafe sex.

Acute, temporary depression is also known as *reactive* or *situational depression*. In everyday language, this describes a reasonably understandable depressive reaction to life events. If your partner is clearly grieving and melancholic after the breakup of a relationship, the loss of a job, or even his team's breakdown in the Super Bowl—and he is neither severely debilitated nor afflicted for more than six months—

this category applies. Many people get through this kind of depression without treatment, but for many others therapy and/or medication can help them feel better. This category specifically rules out bereavement depression, because it is so normal to be depressed when grieving the loss of a loved one. But the intensity and duration of the low mood can reach levels where it would qualify as "beyond normal" and meet the criteria for one of the previously defined clinical categories of depression (even in the case of bereavement).

Other Types of Depression

Seasonal depression, often called seasonal affective disorder (SAD), is a depression that occurs each year at the same time, usually starting in fall or winter and ending in spring or early summer. It is more than just the winter blues or cabin fever. People who suffer from SAD have many of the common signs of depression: sadness, anxiety, irritability, loss of interest in their usual activities, withdrawal from social activities, and inability to concentrate. They often have symptoms such as extreme fatigue and lack of energy, increased need for sleep, craving for carbohydrates, and increased appetite and weight gain. This illness is more commonly seen in people who live at high latitudes (geographic locations farther north or south of the equator), where seasonal changes are more extreme. It is estimated that nearly 10 percent of Alaska residents suffer from SAD, but most of you who live in more moderate climates with a reasonable amount of sunlight may have to search elsewhere to understand the sources of your partner's depression. The influence of latitude on SAD strongly suggests that it is caused by changes in the availability of sunlight. One theory is that with decreased exposure to sunlight, the biological clock that regulates mood, sleep, and hormones is delayed, running more slowly in winter. Exposure to light may reset the biological clock.

Another category of depression that should not be overlooked is **depression secondary to a medical condition**. This would include reactions to medications (including steroids) that were primarily generated by a physiological condition—not a psychological reaction to the idea of suffering from this physical condition. Medical illnesses such as strokes, heart attacks, thyroid imbalances, and Parkinson's disease are all known to be risk factors for precipitating depression. Although many depression symptoms can benefit from psychological understanding and interventions, depression in these cases probably will not abate very much until the source of this physiological problem is treated.

Male hormonal depression, also known as *male menopause, andropause, male climacteric,* or *testosterone-deficiency depression,* sometimes begins to insidiously take hold during the male aging process (Diamond 1997). This is the only form of depression that we've reviewed so far that, by definition, only applies to men. Although, as for women, the male response to aging and hormone changes has very little consistent pattern, sometime during a man's fourth or fifth decade of life (and sometimes as early as his thirties), his body's production of testosterone may begin to slow. The gradual decline can produce a variety of changes and effects on the male body:

- Erectile dysfunction

- Decreased libido (low sex drive)

- Mood disturbances, including depression, irritability, and feeling tired

- Loss of muscle size and strength

- Osteoporosis (bone thinning)

- Increased body fat

- Difficulty with concentration and memory loss

- Sleep difficulties

MALE DEPRESSION AND YOUR RELATIONSHIP

This book is about the interaction between the different varieties of male depression and intimate relationships. Before you can figure out how to best intervene, offer support, and take care of yourself, you must understand what you (and he) are dealing with and how this affects your relationship.

Breakdowns in Intimacy

Intimacy—whether it's laughing over a private joke in a restaurant or making love in the bedroom—is a quiet but devastating casualty of depression. When your partner is depressed, he is usually compelled to harness all his resources just to take care of himself and get through the day. It doesn't matter whether he is basically a self-centered person to start out with. The state of depression just doesn't leave much left over for intimate relationships.

If you are in a relationship with a depressed man, you have a bird's-eye view of what he's going through and how your previous connections are unraveling. It can be very difficult to stay connected when your partner is not offering much and isn't treating you very well. In his challenge to make sense out of and handle his depression, he is very likely to transfer his inner pain to something or someone outside himself: you.

Breakdowns in Communication

Problems in relationships are a trigger for depression, and depressed men are frequently unable or unwilling to talk about their sadness. They are often handicapped in their ability to label their feelings accurately, showing instead a sullen irritability, impatience, crankiness, and anger—especially toward the people they are closest to. This, in turn, makes it harder for you, as his partner, to offer the emotional support and guidance that he needs. This unfortunate dynamic can set in motion a downward spiral that typically ends in constant arguments and alienation—and sometimes divorce.

Crises in a family or in a relationship sometimes have the power to bring people together—and often have the devilish power to drive a wedge between them. When you're on the receiving end of anger, blame, or dependency, it can be very difficult to maintain your fundamental compassion and your connection. You may try diligently and lovingly to maintain an open heart, but you still feel emotionally beat up in the process and hardly able to maintain your best and most loving behavior on a consistent basis. It takes a lot to stay connected during these times, and sometimes it taxes you beyond your capacity. You can feel abandoned, confused, frustrated, and fearful about the future, and you may resent the extra burdens you have to bear as a result of what your partner is going through.

Emotional and Sexual Withdrawal

Your depressed partner is likely to withdraw from you and others, reducing the opportunities for the positive benefits of engaging in the world of people. His behavior often becomes increasingly thorny and just plain unattractive (there's no getting around this basic fact: depressed people are not as attractive or appealing as people who are not depressed), generating the self-fulfilling prophecy of social rejection.

Not to mention the fact that he becomes uninterested in sex, can't function as well, or desperately pushes for more sex in a misguided and ill-fated effort to feel good. These patterns all have the potential to alienate you from him, and vice versa. You need to understand and anticipate these reactions, giving you the broadest range of options for how to respond, both internally and interpersonally. The chapters ahead will guide you through these options.

SUMMARY

Now you have an understanding of what typical overt male depression looks like. Although men are much less likely than women to admit it to themselves or to others, you can identify classic symptoms that tell you that some sort of depression has taken hold. By understanding these features, you are in a better position to make sense of what you are observing and ultimately to respond intelligently to what your partner is going through. The next chapter will take you further into the world of male depression, specifically focusing on the hidden forms of male depression that can be even more difficult to recognize, make sense of, and cope with.

Chapter 2

Male-Type Depression: The Guy Who Doesn't Look Depressed

In addition to the patterns of typical depression described in the previous chapter, we now know about a pattern of depressive experiences and behaviors that can only be properly labeled as "male-type depression." This is depression that really looks different in men than in women. In this pattern, men do not usually report sadness, but they do report feeling irritable or tremendously fatigued. They don't have a name for the feelings, but there's a sense of being dead inside. Something is missing. They feel restless, agitated, and unsatisfiable. They lose their vitality. Vague, persistent physical symptoms show up, like headaches, mysterious pain, and insomnia. These men often attempt to "self-medicate" with potentially addictive behaviors like alcohol or drug use, gambling, sexual affairs, workaholism, and reckless physical risk taking. In typical male fashion, they act out rather than turn within. And, most disturbingly for you, they blame others for their vague feelings of unhappiness and for their bad moods.

MALE-TYPE DEPRESSION DEFINED

To put it very simply, women tend to think and process their feelings when they are depressed, and men tend to act. A man who takes action in the face of depression can either be extremely adaptive (such as going out to look for a job if he is feeling depressed about being unemployed) or extremely maladaptive (such as picking a fight and getting drunk to escape feeling bad about himself). Research studies report that when women describe what they actually do when they are depressed, they say, "I try to find out why I feel the way I do," or "I try to analyze my mood" (Nolen-Hoeksema 1993). For men, the patterns are typically quite different. Most men report that they turn to an activity they enjoy or simply decide to distract themselves from the bad feelings: "I decide not to concern myself with my mood." Of course, many people (especially men) are likely to respond with "What do you mean, depressed?"

Seligman concludes that "men and women experience mild depression at the same rate, but in women, who dwell on the state, the mild depression escalates; men, on the other hand, dissolve the state by distracting themselves, by action or perhaps by drinking it away" (1998, 87). While distraction can come in very handy, this particularly male pattern of avoiding uncomfortable emotional states often leads to avoidance, denial, minimization, and acting out. The distress is there, but it remains unnamed and unclaimed.

This reluctance to face up to depression makes life especially difficult for people like me, who are trying to help men get through it, and for people like you, who have to live with it.

Many researchers and theorists who focus on male depression syndrome have tried to identify the central patterns that characterize this long-standing but only recently understood condition (Pollack 1998a; Real 1997). These patterns cluster into four main categories of behavior patterns: discontent with self, antagonism and blame, exaggerated behavior, avoidance and escape. Please note that some of these patterns set the stage for one or more of the other ones. And it is important to remember that these patterns might overlap with more traditional symptoms usually seen in typical overt depression (like despondency, pessimism, low self-esteem, sleep and appetite disturbances, etc.). But they are just as likely to stand on their own: desperate attempts to fend off the core, underlying, unnamed, unacceptable depression.

DISCONTENT WITH SELF

One of the primary features you are likely to see in your partner's male-type depression is a profound unhappiness with himself. He is likely to display signs of the following patterns.

Harsh Self-Criticism

While a moderate dose of self-criticism comes in very handy for all of us, excessive levels corrupt good judgment.

Paul had been married to Celine for twenty years. He was fifteen years older than she; they were sixty-four and forty-nine when they first came into my office, demoralized by several years of arguing, distress, and alienation from each other. Paul had been a successful attorney until a few years earlier, when he had a mild stroke that slowed him down considerably. His mood and self-image, never particularly solid to begin with, crashed with the stroke and the resultant anxiety, lifestyle changes, and fears about the future.

Celine was vibrant, energetic, and very emotional. She watched as her husband's mood and energy deteriorated right before her eyes. He ruminated about his failures as a provider or protector. She alternately was patient and enraged by his increased recklessness with business investments and extravagant spending. Two years earlier, he had made a disastrous business investment with an irresponsible and exploitative partner whom she had warned Paul about. This history made Celine feel like she couldn't trust Paul, which further undermined their relationship.

As Paul withdrew, paralyzed by his own shame and self-criticism, Celine became more emotional and demanding of his time, his attention, and his common sense. She looked and felt crazier and crazier.

Shamed for Feeling Depressed

Many men, despite their increasing internal distress, feel shamed not only by their perceived failures but by the concept of being depressed.

I worked with Paul and Celine as a couple for a few months without making much progress. In the sessions, Paul adamantly denied that he was depressed and that his behavior patterns were anything to worry about. He stiffened when either of us even hinted at the possibility that he was suffering from the "D-word." Paul insisted that everything was going to be just fine if everyone would just leave him alone. His moods and behavior said otherwise, of course, but it was clear that the very possibility that he might be a "victim of depression" or "suffering from depression" or "weakened by depression" added an unbearable component of diminished masculinity to his self-image. Meanwhile, Celine pleaded. Celine was patient. Celine was angry.

One day Celine called me in tears, saying, "Paul told me he wants a divorce! He won't say why. He has packed up his bags and moved out, and he won't talk to me." A few days later, Paul told Celine, "I just want to spare you having to deal with me. I want to release you because pretty soon I'm going to be drooling in a wheelchair and you need to live your life."

Paul was shamed by his self-image of being a failure as a husband. He felt like he was losing at the game of life. But he couldn't talk about it. He couldn't label it for what it was. He couldn't call it temporary, or based on circumstances, or something that did not overtake his entire personality or self-worth. He could only run. And, at one point when I tried to empathize with his life situation by suggesting that he was depressed and could benefit from antidepressant medication, he scoffed and never returned.

Imaginary Crimes

Sometimes the source of shame-based depression is the experience of unconscious guilt. According to *control-mastery theory*, also known as *imaginary crimes*, children often grow up believing that they have committed some emotional crime against their family or that they are at risk for doing so (Weiss and Sampson 1986; Engel and Ferguson 1990). The perception of having committed these crimes leads them to feel shame. And shame, as we know, rarely leads to anything good. More often, shame generates rage, projection of blame, depression, self-destructive behavior, and defensive reactions.

Deon, a man with a tragic past, told me this story of his imaginary crimes:

> When I was little, I desperately tried to save my mother as she fought off the cancer that finally killed her. She lasted four years. I ended up with this script that said, "You really have to help fix this woman in your life." Now, in my relationships, I've ended up choosing wounded woman who needed a lot of help, and kept trying to fix them. But I also kept getting mad at them because they would not get fixed. And they have always complained because I seemed moody, unhappy, and unsatisfiable. The sad thing is, they were right.

The crimes referred to here are truly imaginary, because most reasonable observers would say that it is not fair for the child to take on the burden of guilt in this situation. Deon's depression and sense of failure haunted all his attempts at future relationships.

ANTAGONISM AND BLAME OF OTHERS

The covert, underlying depression that these men experience, when unnamed and unclaimed, often leads down a dangerous path of blame. The depression feels so fundamentally unmasculine and threatening that it must be defended against at all costs. This spells trouble for those close to these men.

Demanding Respect from Others

Take Stuart as an example of this tricky dynamic. Stuart was a client of mine who brought his family in because of all the problems he and his wife were having with their kids. Stuart was in his late forties and had a history of depression, which he'd treated by taking Prozac off and on for several years. Stuart had lost a leg during combat in Vietnam and had struggled for decades with VA hospitals and clinics trying to find the right prosthesis. He worked in the administration of a small business and was pretty low on the totem pole. His bouts of depression were marked with profound feelings of helplessness and powerlessness, which he usually masked by trying to take bold actions.

In one session, Stuart and his family talked about the drama of the past week. Stuart had come home to find his daughter, Karen, in tears, wailing (as only a thirteen-year-old girl can wail) about how an alleged friend had spread rumors of her sexual behavior at a party. Stuart—being a good dad who cared about his daughter and couldn't bear to see her in such pain—sprang into action. He single-handedly decided that the solution was to call the other girl's mother and insist that her daughter apologize to Karen and tell the other kids that she just made the story up. Stuart's daughter's response to this was a resounding "Noooooooooooooooo!"

When his wife politely said that she didn't think this was a good plan, Stuart went ballistic. He demanded that they follow his plan and insisted that, if they didn't, it meant that he was not a valuable or respected member of the family. His only recourse then would be to leave. When no one responded, perhaps too stunned to know what to say, Stuart packed his bags and left. He spent the night at a motel and then came back the next morning feeling stupid.

In the family session, Stuart was able to articulate what had set off this tantrum: "I felt like I had to take charge. Nobody listens to me anymore! I started thinking that I would be unloved and disrespected if I couldn't make a difference here. It was all about feeling powerless. I guess I kind of forgot that we were *all* feeling powerless. We were all in this together."

Stuart, feeling powerless without the capacity to name it and claim it, could only respond by "puffing up." Even good men with good values who deeply care about their kids and family can mismanage their reactions to everyday family events when they are struggling with underlying or covert depression. They tend to get tripped up by emotions that they can't handle very well. They feel helpless and powerless, which is constitutionally intolerable for most of us raised as boys and men. So they insist on implanting solutions and react impatiently and even aggressively when their solutions aren't respected or implemented, or if they prove to be ineffective.

As author Terrence Real says, "The pattern in males of moving from the helpless, depressed, 'one down' position to a transfigured, grandiose, 'one up' position has become one of the most powerful and ubiquitous narratives of our time" (1997, 68).

Rick, a successful businessman who had always complained of restlessness and dissatisfaction with his life, was spending time with his wife and her family. He had always felt devalued and disrespected by his in-laws, and on this occasion (not unlike many others) he desperately tried to inflate and impress. He name-dropped about important people he knew, relentlessly steered the conversation back to his material success, and dispensed unsolicited financial advice. His wife was horrified and later told him he had acted like a fool. In short, Rick's depressive view of himself had been activated, prompting him to go on the offensive with an obvious and embarrassing ploy to gain respect.

Increased Antagonism: The Best Defense Is a Good Offense

A man who is struggling with depression, particularly this form of covert male depression, lives in dread of experiencing even more of it. At some level, usually not consciously, he recognizes that his capacity to handle more dysphoria is limited. His emotional survival depends on fending off experiences that will make him feel worse about himself or more hopeless about the future. In these situations, the best defense seems like a good offense. When he smells danger—as in situations that might activate some feeling of depression—he proactively goes on the attack.

My client Antonio had a history of alcohol abuse in his long-standing marriage. He had recently been busted by his wife for cheating on her. They came this close to divorce, but she agreed to try to work on the marriage as long as he took responsibility for his long-standing depression, substance abuse, and occasional infidelity. Antonio had hit rock bottom. He was deeply depressed and anguished about the damage he had done and the impending losses he faced if he did not shape up.

But in a classic effort to avoid even more feelings of worthlessness and guilt, Antonio managed to make the situation his wife's fault. When she would bring up her fears and anger, Antonio found ways to make her feel bad about bringing up the subject. It was always the wrong timing, or the wrong tone of voice, or excessively repetitious. Why? Because her pain reminded him of his depression and the helplessness he felt to undo the damage. Instead, he attacked her. Because this strong, bold, powerful man was scared by his own depression, he felt compelled to strike out at the victim of his misbehavior.

Attacking When Hurt

Sometimes the covertly depressed man will generate conflicts with his partner that seem to come out of nowhere—although they usually can be traced to some way that he has felt hurt or threatened.

In the movie *Good Will Hunting*, the main character is a young man named Will who is haunted by an abusive past and a terror of being exposed as "damaged goods." When the new love of his life, the first woman whom he has ever begun to open up to and trust, invites him to move to California with her, he goes rigid—and eventually ballistic.

In terror that he will trust her and then be rejected because of his profound flaws and inadequacies, he coldly attacks her. This offense is capped by the ultimate blow of the depressed man who goes on the offensive: "I don't love you." On the surface, Will shows nothing that we would typically describe as signs of depression, but he is the poster child for the male-type depression pattern of a man going on the offensive when he feels like he is on the defensive.

Suspicion and Mistrust

Another form of blaming and antagonistic behavior is expressed through suspiciousness and mistrust. Locked into these patterns of covert, unnamed depression, your partner may feel all-too-easily threatened and insecure. Instead of talking about it or trying to make sense of it, he attacks and blames and retaliates. Shakespeare's Othello, an insecure and vulnerable man, lives in dread that his wife, Desdemona, will betray him. With nasty assistance from a scheming friend, Othello starts to think of Desdemona as someone who is untrustworthy. Then everything she does (her handkerchief suspiciously missing, an overheard conversation that could imply her infidelity) just further serves to confirm what he has come to believe about her. There is no possibility of doubt; he cuts her no slack. His profound pessimism about the inevitability that he will be rejected and betrayed leads him to see it where it does not exist in a futile attempt to ward off the even greater injury of being surprised and crushed even further.

This pattern, like many other interpersonal patterns of the defended depressed man, generates a self-fulfilling prophecy of rejection and betrayal. But it is important to understand where it all comes from, because many men actually are capable of changing this pattern when they learn to recognize it and its consequences. And many of you can find ways to help him make these changes if you understand it, too.

EXAGGERATED BEHAVIOR

Hidden depression in men, even if it only barely leaks through into consciousness, presents a profound and intolerable threat to traditional masculinity. In response, many men unconsciously turn to exaggerated, hypermasculine behaviors. It's as if they have to consistently prove to themselves and everyone else that they're really not depressed, not weak, not vulnerable—not emasculated. It's as if they are desperately performing masculinity so they can scoff at the notion of depression, in effect saying to everyone, "Look at me. Do I look like a guy who's depressed?"

Although many people of both genders live interesting and exc[it]ing lives by taking risks and seeking out stimulating life experie[nces] covertly depressed guy will often turn desperately to stimulating experiences to try to shock himself out o[f] He hates feeling bored. He hates feeling down. [He] and empty and deadened inside. So he uncon[sciously] electro-convulsive therapy to himself by engaging i[n] experiences.

Substance Abuse

For some men, this shows up in an obvious way: substance abuse. Depressed men are quite likely to drink to excess. And they are especially attracted to stimulants like cocaine, crystal methedrine, or Ritalin. This is a form of self-medication and, unfortunately, it sort of works. These drugs provide a buffer to the dysphoria so that, following the essential principles of learning theory, the reinforcing effect leads him back to repeat the same behaviors, despite the long-term cost. When he is depressed enough, just like when he is in chronic pain, he can get pretty desperate, and he is quite susceptible to trying anything to convince himself that what he is doing is justifiable and good.

Anger Addiction

Current brain research adds another dimension to why someone would engage in a pattern of blaming, angry, and sometimes explosive behavior: his body and brain may be getting a real charge from it. What we now know more clearly than ever before is that anger can make someone feel powerful—not just psychologically, but *neurochemically*. It is, for many men, a magic potion that can lift them out of pain, self-doubt, and depression.

First of all, the brain secretes norepinephrine when a person feels provoked. Norepinephrine produces an analgesic-like effect: it deadens pain. To make the cocktail even more potent, the angry brain also secretes the amphetamine-like hormone epinephrine. This allows the depressed man to experience a surge of energy throughout his body. This accounts for the adrenaline rush that so many people report feeling during a sudden attack of anger.

People who are drawn to angry outbursts and other temper explosions often have an understimulated nervous system (Foreman 2000). In these cases, outbursts may actually provide the rush of energy that jolts the brain to more normal functioning. Has the man in your life ever gone out looking for a fight? Some men experience this walking into a bar or a party. And others arrive home and walk in the door ated and restless. He sees you or the kids and Mr. Hyde emerges. s desperately searching for something to be pissed off about.

There's always something. And when he finds the excuse he is looking for, he blows up. He is addicted to anger, because it lifts him (but only temporarily) out of depression and gives him the jolt of energy he craves. It is his cocaine. And it always seems like it is justified and someone else's fault.

Too Much Sex

Sex can provide the same effect as anger, and can likewise mask the underlying engine that generates the urge: covert depression. For instance, George came into my office and told me the story of his compulsive philandering. He had been married to Andrea for five years, the last two of which had been colored by a torrid affair he had conducted with a sales rep who worked at his business:

> My escapades with her were so hot, I would sneak out any chance I could get. I would get up early in the morning, tell Andrea I was going to the gym, and sneak over for a quickie. Finally, my lover got tired of it. She knew I was trying to use her to self-medicate. She told me that it was too much pressure to be responsible for my unhappiness.

That's it in a nutshell. George had turned over the responsibility for managing his unhappiness to his sexual escapades with his lover. Now, months after the affair was over, months after his wife found out, it suddenly dawned on him:

> I realize now that I have been depressed, off and on, for years. And I keep turning to other people and activities to bail me out. I think that's why I got married in the first place, for the rush, and why I lost interest in the marriage. I wasn't getting the endorphin rush any more, and I needed to get it somewhere.

It may be difficult to think of highly active, risk-taking, angry, sexually active men as being depressed. But many are. And when they can recognize that and take responsibility for it, then they—and the relationship they are in—might actually get real.

AVOIDANCE AND ESCAPE

When you know that your husband or boyfriend is acting erratically, withdrawing emotionally, or making crummy decisions to prove to others that he is a strong and independent person—in other words, when you know that he is going through male-type depression—you are probably observing a pattern of behavior designed to avoid and/or escape feeling bad.

Now, there's certainly nothing inherently wrong with finding a way to avoid or escape feeling bad. It can represent a very resourceful set of skills. But when your partner is feeling depressed, anxious, alienated, lethargic, unmotivated, and pessimistic, he may have a vague awareness that something disturbing is taking place within and feel woefully ill-equipped to recognize it, name it, express it, and productively deal with it. Or at least live with it until it passes. This sets the stage for unhealthy avoidance and escape. Avoidance patterns are evident when he carefully discerns situations that he does not want to find himself in and carves out a lifestyle engineered to avoid them. Psychologically, this make perfect sense. Who wants to put themselves in a situation that is likely to make them feel bad? Except that the life restrictions we are talking about here are crippling.

Defensive Avoidance

Some men systematically—and often unconsciously—refuse to put themselves in situations where they may get hurt or suffer loss. Will Hunting (in the movie *Good Will Hunting*) has carefully crafted such a life. As I described earlier, he turns down the opportunity to move to California with a terrific young woman who loves him. In the big blowout argument with his girlfriend, this deeply (covertly) depressed man, who masks all his unhappiness with activity, bravado, and emotional distancing, screams out at her. He accuses her of just wanting to have a fling with him until she meets somebody else more worthy, someone from her social class. It's clear to the audience that he's acting nuts. And in a way, it is nuts, because he's giving up the very thing he wants out of dread of putting too much trust in another person and then getting devastated by the eventual rejection.

Sadness Phobia

Part of what handicaps Will Hunting is that he is terrified of identifying, naming, acknowledging, and expressing his profound sadness and pain. He cannot grieve for what he has lost and how he has suffered. So, in classic guy style, he sucks it up and projects a tough and impenetrable exterior. The driving force behind these behaviors is his desperation to avoid the possibility of acknowledging emotional pain. When he is able to do this, his male-type depression loosens its grip on him and he develops at least the possibility of a more authentic and intimate relationship.

Escape Behaviors

Many depressed men are desperate to escape emotionally uncomfortable situations. One of the most common ways they remove themselves is emotional zoning out, or what author Terrence Real calls the "I Don't Want to Talk About It" syndrome (1997). A little of this is pretty normal. A lot of it signals an underlying depression and anxiety that can destroy the relationship.

Mikhail's marriage was deteriorating because he kept shutting down emotionally whenever his wife tried to talk to him about anything that could possibly make him feel bad. As Mikhail tried to make sense of this, he recalled his experience growing up with his dad:

> I can remember so clearly being called into my father's den.
> It was always filled with smoke. He sat there in that big
> avocado-green chair, and I was always in that brown chair where
> I had to sit up very straight. And he would lay into me. Lecture
> me. Put me down. It would go on and on for what seemed like
> hours. I just zoned out. And when teachers in school would go
> into lecture mode, I would zone out the same way. It felt like a
> wall kicking into place that insulated me from what I was hearing.
> And the same thing keeps happening with Rosie. It just drives her
> nuts and makes everything worse.

But zoning out isn't the only way depressed men escape. These behaviors run the gamut from overworking to drinking, surfing the

or having affairs. For example, my client Lane told
ated he felt in his relationship with his wife:

> telling me that she is tired of me rejecting her and
> She tells me I'm just a "taker." So what do I do?
> rink too much. I zone out on the Internet. I try to
> occupy my time without too much thought. I don't know what to
> do, so I do nothing. I can't do anything right.

The drive for emotional self-protection makes sense psychologically. But it is corrosive to the self and ultimately corrosive to the
relationship.

EXERCISE: Is Your Partner Secretly Depressed?

Below is a questionnaire for you to fill out to help you assess whether
the man in your life is suffering from male-type depression. In the
right-hand column, score 0 if the item is not a problem, 1 if it is something of a problem, and 2 if it is very noticeable or serious.

Please note that a few of the items on this inventory are similar to
the depression questionnaire in chapter 1. These two patterns of male
depression are not completely separate—they share some fundamental
features of depression, no matter the differences in how these problems
show up behaviorally.

Is Your Partner Secretly Depressed?	Score 0, 1, or 2
DISCONTENT WITH SELF	
1. Does he subject himself to very harsh self-criticism?	
2. Does he seem very sensitive to the possibility of being shamed or looking bad?	
3. Does he have a very limited vocabulary to describe his feelings?	
4. Does he avoid putting himself in situations where it might appear that he is failing?	

ANTAGONISM AND BLAME OF OTHERS	
5. Does he blame others for his bad moods?	
6. Does he demand respect without behaving so as to earn respect?	
7. Does he think all of his problems would end if only you would behave differently?	
8. Is he guarded and suspicious?	
9. Does he have frequent angry outbursts?	
EXAGGERATED BEHAVIOR	
10. Does he crave sex desperately?	
11. Is he (or has he been) having an affair?	
12. Does he abuse substances, TV, video games, or the Internet to self-medicate?	
13. Does he engage in high-risk behaviors (driving fast, inappropriate flirting, reckless business ventures, etc.)?	
14. Is he a workaholic?	
15. Is he compulsive about time and order?	
16. Is he perfectionistic?	
AVOIDANCE AND ESCAPE	
17. Does he have difficulty grieving when he suffers a loss or disappointment?	
18. Does he suffer from the "I Don't Want to Talk About It" syndrome? Does he express feelings of worthlessness? Does he seem especially discouraged about the future?	
19. Does he shy away from hearing about your problems because they might bring him down? Does he complain that everything is going wrong no matter how hard he's trying?	
20. Does he insist that everything is okay, even when it is obvious that it's not?	
SCORE	

This is not a scientific tool for proper diagnosis, so I won't offer an absolute cutoff for determining male-type depression. But the exercise should give you a guideline to help you determine if your partner is covertly depressed. If you discover that he is, you can help him deal with this—or at least you can make more sense of what you are going through and cope with it better. Any score of 10 or above suggests male-type depression, and anything over 20 should serve as a major red flag. Please remember that this measures only one cluster of depression symptoms—male-type depression or covert depression—and the more familiar signs of depression are addressed in chapter 1.

SUMMARY

Male-type depression represents a pattern of male depression that doesn't usually fit our traditional picture of what a depressed person is supposed to look like. We see four basic clusters of behavior patterns: discontent with self, antagonism and blame others, exaggerated behavior, and avoidance and escape. These patterns are all generated by the difficulty that many men have in identifying their internal experiences and in dealing with the negative self-image associated with depression. The more you know about these signs of underlying depression, the more you can plan how to respond.

CHAPTER 3

Connecting with a Depressed Guy

Everything about depression leads men to feel shame, to minimize the way they feel, and to deny there is anything wrong. Most self-respecting, red-blooded American guys cannot tolerate the sense of psychological impotence that generally accompanies depression. Impotence, of course, is the dirtiest word in the language for most men.

So even though the man in your life is depressed, he may not allow himself to admit it. There are two main factors that join forces to create this condition: the first is that many men do not recognize their feelings very well, and the second is that men have trouble admitting to anything smacking of weakness. And depression is associated with weakness.

In this chapter, you will learn the best ways to respect these forces and how to successfully connect with the emotions and experiences of your partner in language that he is more likely to hear.

)OESN'T KNOW WHAT

guess." This was the reply of my client Carlo when
what was wrong. He probably said this same sentence
five hundred times in response to her repeated pleading that he talk to
her about his moods, his emotional withdrawal, his drinking, and
ultimately, his infidelity.

Feelings That Have No Words

In Greek, *lexis* means "word" and *thymus* means "emotion."
Combined with the prefix *a*, meaning "not" or "without," the lexicon
of psychiatry has generated the word *alexithymia*. Alexithymia literally
means lacking the words or labels for the experience of emotions. True
alexithymics just seem different, as if they are operating on a different
social planet from everybody else.

Ron Levant (1998) coined the term "normative male
alexithymia" to describe a widespread phenomenon in our culture.
Although it may not reach the level of clinically significant proportions
like bona fide alexithymia, it still captures a "condition" that plagues
men in relationships. The term describes mildly (or sometimes more
severely) depressed men who struggle to identify their inner states.

Many male-type depressed men rely only on their cognitive
descriptions, analyses, and opinions to make sense of themselves and
their relationships. Because of this gap in self-awareness, many men are
prevented from utilizing the simplest and most effective method for
dealing with complex feelings and difficult moods: identifying, thinking
about, and expressing a wide range of feelings. These are skills in
emotional intelligence that women tend to be able to do better. If you
consistently feel as if you just can't get through to the man you're
involved with, it may be that he lacks these emotional skills. He may
simply not be reading your cues or speaking your language. He is not
actively lying, avoiding, or denying—he just doesn't understand what
you are talking about or how you want him to respond.

The problem is not that normative male alexithymics don't really
feel anything. It's just that they are not very good at making the
connections between stressful events and distressing emotions and

dysfunctional behaviors. They lack the skills to know what their feelings are, and they are especially unable to put their feelings into words. This specifically inhibits the ability of many men to properly label the distress, emptiness, anxiety, and pessimism that they are experiencing.

He can't recognize and call his experience depression, or even some other more benign label, if he knows only that he's feeling sort of sluggish or if he notices that other people seem especially irritating.

Crummy Relationship Judgment

In the movie *About Schmidt*, Jack Nicholson plays the lead role of Warren Schmidt, who is recently widowed, lonely, and depressed. But he doesn't know what to call his experience or what to do about it. To the audience, it is plain as day that this man is depressed and lost. You may feel the same way about the man in your life, seeing clearly that something is wrong with him. You see that he is profoundly disconnected from himself and from others. But if you were to suggest this to him, you would likely get a denial and a "No, no, I'll be fine" response. And he would not be purposely lying or deceiving. He really would not have the language to describe his experience or make sense of it in the language that makes sense to you.

In one scene in the movie, Schmidt meets a very nice couple living in a trailer who befriend him. When the man in this couple goes out to pick up something from the store and Schmidt is left alone with the youngish woman, she tells him that he seems sad and lonely. He is touched by her compassion and understanding. He softens and opens up to her. He even puts his head on her shoulder. She is a little surprised. Then he starts kissing her passionately—and she jumps up, outraged, and screams at him to leave. It is so painfully obvious that he is not a sexual predator and means no harm. He is just emotionally clueless. He has had no clue about how depressed he has been, and thus he is overwhelmed with gratitude that a kind soul has identified this pain in his heart. And he is so inexperienced with his emotional life that he confuses friendliness and understanding—and the flood of good feelings that accompany them—with sexual interest. So, because he has a depression with no name, and because he experiences warm feelings of connection with no proper name, he turns this into one of his few known pathways for meaningful connection: sex.

For so many men, their ability to make these kinds of discriminations is poorly developed. They have an underdeveloped capacity to distinguish the different experiences of warmth and closeness, just like their inability to distinguish between irritation and rage, or minor rudeness from profound betrayal and threat.

My client Raul told me about what he went through earlier in his marriage that was chillingly similar:

> *I was so depressed in my marriage. I felt totally disconnected.*
> *I could tell that my wife didn't care for me anymore, and I felt*
> *lost. Then I started to develop a thing for her sister. I couldn't*
> *stop thinking about her. Finally, after I had a few drinks at a*
> *family gathering, I took her aside and told her, "You're the one*
> *I'm really in love with!" She was shocked. She told her mother,*
> *who told my wife, and the shit started rolling. It was just like*
> *in the Woody Allen movie* Hannah and Her Sisters. *It was like*
> *I was on drugs, except the drug was depression. It set the stage*
> *for me to lose all judgment and do something so stupid and totally*
> *passive-aggressive.*

The depression here—unnamed and unclaimed—serves as a profound disinhibitor. It releases the man to do things that he would not normally do, because he desperately wants to find some salvation from the feelings that are so disorganizing.

But if he can be drawn out of the alexithymia and actually put some words to his feelings (all the feelings, not just anger or blame), there is hope that he may quit projecting responsibility for his unhappiness onto you.

GUIDELINES FOR TALKING FEELINGS WITH MEN

So what are you supposed to do when you see these issues at work in your partner? It is never your responsibility to provide an emotional life for him, but there are lots of things you can do to help the two of you communicate in a common language.

Respect different languages. It is very important that you respect the basic truth: the man you love may not speak the same language that you do. He feels feelings, but may not always know what to call them. He may want to have just as great and meaningful a relationship as you do, but he may have a different style or tolerance level for processing emotions. This is okay. Unless the disparity is extreme, talking about psychological states in the same language is not necessary for a success-ful relationship. If you pressure him to be like you, you will lose him further.

Remember what is most important. On the other hand, you should expect, demand (and offer) respect, fundamental good will, genuine affection, and reliable behavior. Plus a little healthy chemistry.

A little feeling goes a long way. Be satisfied with feeling words that, to you, may seem like a trivialization of his actual experience. Any-thing that helps open the window to the world of feelings is moving in the right direction.

She: I could tell how much trouble you had sleeping last night. You must be really scared about what's going to happen with all the layoffs at work.

He: Scared? No. I've got it down. I have a plan either way.

She: I know. I believe in you. But it's only human to be a little worried about it. That's probably what's getting in the way of a good night's sleep.

He: Yeah, I do worry a little, I guess.

Educate about feelings. Gently suggest feeling words to apply to what he is going through, based on your own experiences or knowledge of him. Remember that, as a man, he is less likely to have developed as rich a vocabulary for different feeling words as you have. He may need some coaching. Try not to get mad or cop an attitude because he doesn't already know how to do this.

She: I thought the way your dad made fun of you last night was pretty mean. How did that make you feel?

He: I don't know. I'm just used to it.

She: I would have felt embarrassed. And then pretty resentful.

He: Embarrassed. I never thought about that. I guess I was kind of embarrassed. He does that a lot, doesn't he?

Use his language. Communicating always works better when you genuinely try to speak the other person's language, using his images, metaphors, and life experience. If your partner is a sports nut, you should talk to him about leading sports figures who have acknowledged problems. If he thinks as a businessman, point out to him how effectively he uses consultants in his work and how little he worries about appearing weak as a result.

She: I just read this article about Terry Bradshaw dealing with years of depression—and he won four Super Bowls! It's okay for you to be going through this, too, you know.

The power of kids. If you're ever stumped for how to get a man to dip into his emotions more deeply, bring up the subject of his kids. Many men who are extremely out of touch with tender emotions in most areas of their lives can be easily brought to tears when they focus on how their kids feel, how much they worry about their kids, or how much their kids mean to them. It also may be helpful to gently bring up how, as a dad, he may be affecting the kids when he acts in destructive ways, or how determined he's always been not to make some of the mistakes that his own parents made with him. If he doesn't have kids, ask him to think about his younger sibling or anyone else who may look up to him.

She: I know you keep telling me that you don't think you have a problem, but both David and Lauren have told me that they're worried about you. I know how much you love them—they really need you to do something.

He: Maybe you're right. For them.

"WHAT ARE YOU TALKING ABOUT? I'M NOT DEPRESSED!"

I just wanted to wait it out. I knew that I couldn't be going through something like this. I was a strong guy. And I didn't want anyone to know what I was feeling inside.

Like my client Dennis, above, hiding bad feelings is very common in most men. Since men traditionally have felt so much pressure to maintain an attitude of competence, independence, and emotional invulnerability, the tendrils of depression—even covert depression—can seem impossibly incongruent and unacceptable. The bugaboo is shame, and since so many men are "shame-o-phobic," the avoidance of acknowledging and expressing feelings of shame makes perfect psychological sense.

Author Terrence Real puts it this way: "One of the ironies about men's depression is that the very forces that help create it keep us from seeing it. Men are not supposed to be vulnerable. Pain is something we are to rise above" (1997, 22).

The Boy Code

Ever since childhood, men have been exposed to what William Pollack (1998b) refers to as the "Boy Code." This code, written nowhere but understood everywhere, insists that boys be stoic, stable, and independent. They should be bold, adventurous, and take risks. They should achieve status, dominance, and power. They must act as if everything is under control, and, perhaps most crippling, they must not reveal feelings or express themselves in such a way as to appear "feminine." Violations of any of the central precepts of the Boy Code often lead to ridicule and the experience of shame. And once shamed, boys are extremely unlikely to venture into the dangerous territory again. Most boys will incorporate these values not only as social and psychological survival mechanisms, but as truths about the way the world is and should be for other men and for their own sons.

Emotional Shutdown

Nelson Mandela describes in his autobiography the intense pressure that he and all boys in his tribe experienced at puberty during the excruciatingly painful rite of circumcision (1994). This is the rite that catapults a boy into true manhood, and it requires enormous powers of pain tolerance and suppression of the truest and most vulnerable emotions. The naked boy is expected to shout out the African cry of

"Ndiyindoda!" at the moment that the knife is wielded. A *boy* would whimper and cry—but a *man* can shout out the word! Mandela hesitated several seconds before shouting "Ndiyindoda!" which caused him great shame. Those few seconds of hesitation were enough to cause him—and, he suspected, the other men observing him—to doubt his readiness for manhood. There is very little room for error or opportunity to step outside the box of the Boy Code.

This is the code that generates situations like that in the scene from *Good Will Hunting* in which Will Hunting (Matt Damon) and his best buddy, Chuckie (Ben Affleck), talk about what has just happened in Will's life. In casual conversation, Chuckie asks Will about how things are going with "your lady." Will tells him casually that she's gone. Neither man shows any display of emotion. After a few grunts and monosyllabic responses, Chuckie uncovers the information that Will's girlfriend has taken off to medical school in California—a week before!

Chuckie sips from his can of beer, raises his eyebrows a little, and responds: "That sucks."

The empty spaces in this guy conversation are deafening. Can you imagine this conversation between two women who are best friends—one week after the fact! Will is emotionally handicapped. He suffers from normative male alexithymia and the restrictions of the Boy Code. Not only is he ill-equipped to properly put a label on what he is feeling, but he is also deathly allergic to acknowledging how much he cares, how much he needs his girlfriend, and how deeply his heart is broken. He is depressed (covert style), but the Boy Code has deeply ingrained in him the prohibition against acknowledging this. It would look too damned weak and needy.

"Real Men" and Depression

In fact, the men who we usually think of as being the toughest—the "real men" who we often turn to for strength and protection—are at an especially high risk for this kind of depression. Soldiers. Firefighters. Police officers. These men utilize traditional male strengths to put aside their fears and rise to the occasion. And thank God for that! But the very strengths that are so invaluable in these emergency situations also inhibit their ability to acknowledge fears, doubts, indecisiveness, or regrets in other types of situations.

Firefighter Jimmy Brown, thirty-seven years old, ran into the World Trade Center minutes after the first plane hit on 9/11 (Hales and Hales 2004). He found himself buried in rubble and ash. He was sure this was the day he would die, but he miraculously survived with only minor physical injuries. The trauma was not over, however. The post-traumatic stress from what he had witnessed and experienced plunged him into an emotional hell and a paralyzing depression. He spent days never leaving the house, then finally, by his wife's insistence, sought out a psychologist and began the emotional healing process. As he began to see himself more clearly, he realized how firefighters and police officers put up a front that they don't need help because they're always helping others. He learned that there's nothing wrong with admitting that something is wrong. Brown is now developing a peer-counseling program to help police and firefighters deal with stress and depression. This doesn't get in the way of doing his "man's job" well. He just has more options now and can turn the defenses off and on when the situation calls for it.

Labeling and Shame: Guy Talk

It's not likely that you will convince the depressed man in your life to identify and express feelings of vulnerability, indecisiveness, and self-doubt by telling him that it is important to get in touch with his feminine side. You're better off calling it (accurately) his "human" side. Even better, the way to help this man find it acceptable to go into this anxiety-provoking territory is to frame it as the most profoundly masculine of tasks. You can help him reframe his male identity, which is a sacred power that you should only use if you genuinely believe that you are acting with sincere motives and in his best interest.

If you tell him that what you are most looking for in a man is someone who is secure enough to talk about his fears and doubts, you may help him learn new lessons about true manhood—and open the door to making peace with the internal, covert depression.

EXERCISE: Validating Your Partner

Try opening up a conversation with your partner that includes telling him the qualities that make you feel closest to him. Give him specific examples of when you have seen these, and let him know how much you would love to see even more of them. Most men are extremely vulnerable to how they are perceived by women. Here are some examples:

1. "Honey, I saw how understanding you were with Emily when she was in such a bad mood last night. I think that really meant a lot to her. I feel really close to you when I see you coming through for her like that."

2. "I can't believe how hard you tried to have a good time out on the dance floor at the party, even though I know you hate dancing. That felt like a gift to me. I love that part of you."

3. "Remember last night, when you told me how worried you felt about living up to your father's expectations? I don't think I have ever felt closer to you. When you are real like that, you're the best."

You will know you're striking pay dirt when he lays aside defensiveness and seems to soften right in front of your eyes.

Masculinity Is Great

The message to him should be that masculinity is great, and that he has plenty of it. Nobody is trying to take any of it away from him or to chop his balls off. You just want the whole package of manhood, not some schoolboy or media-induced caricature. And, in the meantime, you can make it clear that you really need him, and that you can't allow yourself to really need him if you don't know what he is all about.

The only way for any of these proposed changes to make sense for most of you is to frame them in language that does not challenge his (or your) fundamental definitions of male identity. In fact, you need to help activate what is best about masculinity to help him let these changes in thinking, feeling, and acting take root. If you tell your partner how important it is for him to display more emotional vulnerability, he might roll his eyes and harden his defenses. He may reluctantly comply to keep you happy if you insist he go there, but he may not really endorse this new contract.

Male Metaphors: Relational Heroism

Anything you can do to frame the behaviors that you value in language that celebrates his masculinity rather than appears to diminish it has a greater likelihood of success. The notion of "relational heroism" (in which we all have the opportunity to act heroically in the ordinary, everyday choices of our relationship lives) is an example of this. Author Terry Real defines it like this:

> Relational heroism occurs when every muscle and nerve in one's body pulls one toward reenacting one's usual dysfunctional pattern, but through sheer force or discipline or grace, one lifts oneself off the well-worn track toward behaviors that are more vulnerable, more cherishing, more mature. Just as the boyhood trauma that sets up depression occurs not in one dramatic incident, but in transactions repeated thousands of times, so, too, recovery is comprised of countless small victories. (1997, 277)

Being a hero lies at the core of identity for most men. In communicating with your partner, one way to get in the door is to help expand his definition of heroic behaviors. Here's an example of a man (Richard) whose wife helped him discover how to be a hero in their relationship:

> *Kelly wanted to go out dancing. And, as usual, she wanted to dress up and look hot. I know I don't really have any reason to be suspicious or jealous, and I'm trying to work on that. So we go out to this club with a whole bunch of other couples. Kelly starts rocking out, having a great time, getting crazy. I look around at the other men. Half of them—half of us!—are standing around looking sullen and withdrawn. Like they don't fit in, or they're envious that their wives can loosen up and they can't, or they are just uncomfortable trying to dance. And they look like they're pouting.*
> *Now, as a reflection of myself as a man, that doesn't look pretty. So I say, "What the hell?" and I get out on the dance*

*floor and try my best to get into it. I am determined to try to
have fun, and not to look negative or disapproving—like I usually
do. And it feels pretty good.*

*Then Kelly comes over and reaches for me and gives me
one of those long, passionate kisses. The type of kiss that only
comes along once in a while, maybe every few months. Wow!
I don't forget these things!*

*The next day, she says to me, "You seemed to really like
that kiss last night!" I say, "Yeah—what do I have to do to get
more of these?" And she says, "Just be the way you were last
night. You were my hero. That's all it takes."*

That's all it takes? I can do that.

Richard took the leap here—but it was Kelly who provided the
mirror of masculinity. Her response helped him feel like his awkward
dancing and less sullen attitude was a big turn-on for her. Her response
helped him learn more about how to be a whole man.

GUIDELINES FOR TALKING ABOUT DEPRESSION

Call it something else. You don't really have to call it depression, if
that is going to alienate him. You can call it stress, which is a more
male-friendly term. Your goal is not to break through his defenses and
convince him of everything you're sure you know and understand
about him. You have one simple goal—to do anything you can to help
him take some actions that will help him, help you, and help your
relationship.

Labeling can be a relief. As usual, no rule applies in all situations. For
some men, it's just the opposite. These guys respond extremely well to
calling this experience depression, because then they have a label with
an action plan. This can be an enormous relief. The only way that you
know whether labeling will be a relief or if it will be threatening is with
a little trial and error. I have heard conversations in which the woman
casually suggests to the man that it sounds like he's going through a bit
of depression, and his eyes light up, and he says, "You think so? Maybe
you're right!" Whereas another man might reply, "It's not depression, I
just have a lot of stress!" There's your answer.

Make sure he knows what's heroic. Remember that you have a very valuable role in helping to shape your partner's narrative about masculinity. In Pat Conroy's novel *The Great Santini*, a mother writes a letter to her son on his eighteenth birthday and tells him that "I wanted to tell you that gentleness is the quality I most admire in men" (1976, 203). If your partner clearly gets the message from you that telling you about his feelings or taking responsibility for his bad moods are profoundly masculine (and really aren't your attempts at emasculation), you may help him feel like a relational hero.

GUIDELINES FOR TALKING ABOUT DEPRESSION MYTHS

Many of the reasons for denying the problem, keeping it to himself, and not seeking help even when he recognizes that something is wrong stem from long-standing misconceptions men (and many women) have about the nature of depression. Here are some of the most common misconceptions, along with specific guidelines for how you can best respond to them.

Remember to always lead with the positive and affirm what you love about him or agree with him about, even if you end up disagreeing or encouraging him to do something different.

Therapy would be useless. He might say something like, "This depression thing is just biological or biochemical—there's no point in therapy or anything psychological." This is sometimes true, but usually not. Even when problems clearly stem from biochemical disturbances, such as in classic bipolar disorders, psychological interventions can still be a very valuable weapon in the treatment arsenal.

Your response: "I know that what you're feeling may mostly be biological. But these things are all mixed together. We both know that your thinking still gets way too negative and off track sometimes. And all the experts say that thinking like this becomes a habit after a while, even if the primary cause is biochemical. They all recommend getting help on both ends."

Thinking is the problem. This is the opposite of the first point, and may come out in a statement like, "Depression is all in my head." Although this is often true, in the sense that the cognitions (thoughts) and narratives that a man uses have the power to either generate or diminish depression, there are many situations in which the symptoms of depression are clearly traceable to bona fide medical or biological conditions that reflect nothing about the man's strength of character or personal choices in worldview or lifestyle. For example: steroid reactions, diabetes, brain tumors, aftereffects of chemotherapy, fibromyalgia, and testosterone depletion are just a few of the physical conditions that can cause depression.

Your response: "You make it sound like you just made this thing up, and it's not real. First of all, it *is* real, even if it is just in your head. And there are so many physical conditions that can be contributing to it, too. I really want you to check with your doctor to make sure we're not missing some reason for this. I think it's good that you think of it as being in your head, because it means that you can try to change what's going on inside of your head. But I hate to see you using that as a way to blame yourself more or make it seem like it's not a real problem."

Toughing it out will work. This attitude usually sounds something like, "Even if I know I'm depressed, I should be able to slug it out myself, like a man." Most men are raised to be self-sufficient and to know where they are going without asking for directions. So it stands to reason that a man would believe that asking for help—by talking about his feelings with someone—would go against the Boy Code. And since most men have little history with reaching out successfully—in fact, they may have plenty of experience with feeling worse or at least embarrassed when talking about problems or weakness—why should they believe that asking for help makes any sense? The reality is that most people with depression do benefit from some sort of counseling or psychotherapy, with or without medication.

One of the most powerful media messages that actually counteracts this programming is evident in the current wave of ads for erectile dysfunction medication. Rafael Palmiero, a Latino baseball star who has hit over five hundred home runs (and counting), is a spokesmen for Viagra. Levitra uses Mike Ditka, former coach of the Chicago Bears and the New Orleans Saints, who has a reputation for being one of the toughest "man's men" there is. The implicit message to men, of course, is that if Rafael Palmiero and Mike Ditka can acknowledge imperfections in what we usually consider to be the pillars of manhood, so can you! Masculinity is redefined as encompassing the capacity—based on personal security in one's manhood—to recognize that you need help and to go get it.

Your response: "I have no doubts whatsoever about what kind of 'real man' you are! But you know what goes into my definition of being a man? Being willing to ask for directions sometimes. I think a strong man is secure enough to be able to ask for help when he needs it. Haven't you seen all those articles about Terry Bradshaw and his depression, Joe Namath and his drinking problems, and Mike Ditka promoting Levitra? If they're not real men, who is?"

Medication indicates weakness. Your man may say, "Okay, even if this is depression, I shouldn't need a pill as a crutch!" We can all respect this position. And it reflects some of the best qualities of masculinity (independence and determination), along with some of the worst (stubbornness, fear of dependency). But this attitude can often be misguided and limiting.

Your response: "I respect that you feel that way, and I probably would too. But you might want to think about this like diabetes or something. There's no shame in taking insulin if your body needs it. And all the experts in depression say that you should try to do anything that breaks the cycle, or all the habits of depression just sink in deeper and deeper. You can always stop the medication if you don't like it or when you've been better for a while."

HOW TO BEGIN THE "D-WORD" CONVERSATION

In the process of writing this book, I shared an early draft of this chapter with a female colleague. Here was her comment: "For me, one of my main hesitations about talking to my partner about depression would be not knowing the best way to say, 'I think you have a problem.' And if he said, 'No, I don't,' I wouldn't know what to do. What should a partner do? Should you make an appointment to talk? Should you bring it up when he's obviously having problems? What if he says he doesn't want to talk about it or denies it's a problem?"

Some men can handle a straightforward conversation on this subject. These men can respond reasonably well hearing, "Honey, I'm feeling worried about you. You seem more and more stressed out by a lot of things. I think you need some help with this. To me, it looks like you might be going through some kind of depression. Will you go see someone about this just so we can be sure? It would mean a lot to me."

Plenty of other men, however, in accordance with themes of this chapter, may balk. The principles we've examined in this chapter all increase the likelihood of engaging in a reasonably successful conversation on this subject, but you still may be met with resistance. Still, you can keep plugging away, approaching from a different angle. Language is important. Timing is important—the conversation is almost doomed to fail if you approach him when he is upset. If he can't handle the D-word, call it "stress." If he won't acknowledge a global problem, stick with the specific behaviors (withdrawal, drinking, sarcasm, insomnia, workaholism, etc.) that are of concern to you. If he is highly sensitized to looking bad or weak in your eyes, make sure to communicate how much you value him. If he often feels blamed by you, try to catch him when he is acting nondepressed and offering you what you need—then reinforce him for that. If you're not getting through, wait a while and try again later. Many men need some time to get used to the idea.

If you keep trying, and you use every approach you can think of, and you're *still* not getting anywhere, then you should talk to a therapist yourself. This will help for two reasons: it will offer some guidance about how to proceed, and you'll get some emotional support yourself for what you are going through.

HOW TO HELP HIM GET THE HELP HE NEEDS

A lot of men will agree to get treatment for depression or to join you in couples counseling sessions because they agree that there are problems and because they have a reasonable amount of faith that talking about the problems will help. However, plenty of other men are very resistant to the idea, because they don't recognize the problem, because they don't feel comfortable talking about these issues, or because it feels vaguely unmasculine to seek this kind of help.

Although it can be very tempting (because you want to be loving and you don't need any more hassles than absolutely necessary), don't accept his resistance at face value. You know that a man is very likely to say, "I don't need help," or "It won't do any good." This isn't the time to insist that he make some life-changing decision based on his profound realization about the depths of his condition. Let him save face by protesting if he wants, but do whatever you can to get him in to seek help—whatever it takes.

And, in addition to what his doctor or therapist may be telling him, you need to strongly encourage him to remain in treatment until you both see progress. With medication, this is usually a few weeks. With therapy, some people notice a boost right away, while for others it may take a few months. Once he notices changes, he is more likely to stick with it.

Here are some tips to help convince your male partner that getting help from a therapist or a physician makes sense. These are not manipulations. Manipulations apply when you are trying to trick or exploit someone. These are just tried-and-true recommendations for the most effective ways of getting your message across:

- *Remind him that nothing is permanent:* "I would at least like you to give this a fair shot. If you try this for awhile and it's getting nowhere, you can stop."

- *Make sure he has a reasonable amount of control over the situation:* "Do you think you would feel more comfortable going to see a male or female therapist?"

- *Offer to take the initiative:* "I'll call and make the appointment. Let's look at your schedule and figure out the times you're available." Some might call this *enabling* (or allowing him to stay helpless), but sometimes you do what you have to do.

- *Offer a reasonable quid pro quo:* "You've been wanting me to go sailing with you for a long time. I promise to go out sailing with you—with a good attitude—if you'll keep a good attitude about this." One caution: don't let the quid pro quo include anything that you would find distasteful or degrading.

- *If you are pushing for couples counseling, reframe the problem as something that he wants to see changed:* "You know how you've been wanting me to stay on our budget? That's one of the things we can work on in these counseling sessions."

- *Appeal to his sense of commitment to his kids:* "I think the moods you've been in and the ways we've been fighting could be really harmful to our kids, and I know how much you love them. I think we owe it to them to take charge of this." Some men feel too defensive, threatened, or angry to do this for their partners or even for themselves—but they can suck it up to do it for the sake of their kids.

- *Let him know how important this is to you:* "I know how much you care about me and how much it means to you to see me happy. This is something that will really mean a lot to me." Most men are very sensitized to the happiness levels of their wives or girlfriends, and for you to acknowledge this will help him feel valued.

- *Draw a line in the sand:* "I am at the end of my rope with our relationship. I love you, and I desperately want this to work, but if you do not go into counseling or get help with this, I'm leaving." Sometimes this is all you have left. Don't say this unless you absolutely have to, and don't say it unless you really mean it.

SUMMARY

Most men dread not only the experience of depression but also the very idea of it. Depression is associated with experiences of weakness, dependence, and nonmasculinity. The more you realize how much impact this has, the more likely you are to respect his sensitivities and get your message across. It is important to help men identify different emotional states and to defuse these negative associations. It is also in everybody's best interest to be prepared to gently and respectfully dispute your partner's unhelpful myths and worries about male depression.

CHAPTER 4

Communicating with the Depressed Guy

Now you know a lot about male depression in its many different forms and faces. But what are you supposed to do about it when it crops up in your relationship? This chapter will offer you a list of the many possible mistakes you can make, and the many possible gifts that you can offer yourself, him, and your relationship.

First some basic communication guidelines. For those of you who have kids (and especially teenagers), you will notice a striking similarity between some of these principles and the principles parents are guided by when they are at their best with their kids. This is not meant to be demeaning to depressed men. I simply mean that when anyone you are intimately involved with is in a fragile emotional state, your smartest and most compassionate response must be well-informed, conscious, and as respectful as you can possibly manage.

Following is a list of helpful guidelines, each of which we'll explore more fully in the chapter.

COMMUNICATION GUIDELINES

1. **Make sure you understand what the "broken mirror" is all about.** The man in your life is probably very sensitized to any response from you that makes him feel bad about himself. Though you're probably not trying to hurt him, his sensitivity causes him to withdraw and sometimes go on the offensive.

2. **Do not get hooked into reacting to his negative "downer" statements.** These are often almost impossible to deal with, but your response can determine whether they start a major brawl or simply float out harmlessly into the atmosphere. Read between the lines. The specific words are not always going to tell you what he is really thinking, feeling, or meaning. "These have been the worst years of my life" might actually mean "Please reassure me that you love me."

3. **Use active listening.** Reflect back what he is saying. Use feeling words that are part of his language, or at least within reach. Unless specifically asked to do so, do not give advice. People often jump to problem solving or even criticism when they feel anxious. Watch out for this. It may not help the flow of communication.

4. **Do your best to offer positive reinforcement.** We all respond best to praise. When your partner starts to change in the right direction, be very careful not to undermine his direction by complaints about how long this has taken or about how far away he still is from doing it really right.

THE POWER OF THE BROKEN MIRROR

The concept of the *broken mirror* in psychology is very important for you to understand because it will help you know how to respond to the depressed man in your life. It may help you understand about times when you have inadvertently pushed him down or pushed him away—because you did not understand the power of the broken-mirror phenomenon.

The secret about men that a lot of women don't really understand is that men are extremely vulnerable to how they are viewed by women. They may not say it or show it directly, but it is there. So most of you have this power—one that you may never have asked for and that you may not welcome. And it is very important that you are aware of this power so you can use it constructively.

How the Mirror Works

The *mirroring* experience originates from the field of self psychology (Shapiro 1995), where it is identified as the "mirroring selfobject." It is a fundamental process that takes place for all of us in any meaningful relationship in our lives. We look to the response from the other person and observe his or her reaction. Does he smile when he sees me? Does she look interested? Did they laugh at my joke? Did he even notice I was here? Is the class paying attention to what I'm saying? If we read the response as essentially positive, then a positive mirroring experience has taken place.

Receiving these positive responses enhances the experience of *self-cohesion*: feeling solid, together, whole, confident, integrated. The need for self-cohesion is primary. Its origins lie in the original needs between the young child and the most central attachment figure, usually the mother. The child has a compelling need to look into the face of his mother and see, reflected back to him, eyes that say, "You are wonderful" and a smile that says, "You make me happy." The self-psychology theory of normal child development states that all children, at regular points in their development, need validation and acknowledgment from parental figures. These figures serve as the mirroring selfobjects. Over time, if the child experiences these positive interactions, the child develops the capacity to feel pride and take pleasure in his accomplishments—to feel competent, valuable, and worthy of appreciation.

When a child looks into the eyes of his parent and sees reflected back to him a loving and approving look, his basic sense of himself is deeply validated. He feels alive and worthy. When an adult looks into the eyes of his or her partner and sees reflected back a look of love, delight, and profound respect, he or she likewise feels alive and worthy.

This process is, of course, not any fundamentally different for women than it is for men. It's just that men are typically less aware of how powerful these needs are and more likely to withdraw or act out when the needs are not met. And men give a special power to their romantic partners to validate their self-worth.

The Broken-Mirror Phenomenon

The reflection you can offer is especially powerful. Many men are very sensitized to signals that might suggest that they are unappreciated, unneeded, or unsuccessful. When the positive mirroring responses are not forthcoming (or at least when he perceives that they are not forthcoming), he may be unable to maintain his sense of self-worth, self-esteem, or personal value.

If your partner was short-changed in the positive-mirroring department growing up, or if he is plagued with self-doubts, or if he is especially attached to maintaining a strong masculine self-image, then he is even more likely than the rest of us to react to perceived broken mirrors.

My client Daniel got to the point where he could clearly recognize some of the ways in which he was most vulnerable to the broken mirror in his relationship with his wife, Natalie:

The one thing that is almost certain to set me off is to hear that I am failing at something. And the two things that I care most about, that are most wrapped up with my identity as a man, are my abilities as a father and my success in my profession. So, one thing Natalie does that really sets me off is when she tells me that I don't care about my kids. Those are fighting words. An uncaring dad is the last thing I want to be, and she is the person whose opinion on this subject matters the most.

Sometimes people (both men and women) say really nasty things designed to make their partners feel awful. Natalie was not one of these women. She would just get mad at Daniel sometimes when she saw him being self-centered and she would hurl the "You don't care about the kids" accusation. As Daniel describes, this reflected back a picture of himself that cut him deeply. When he was plagued with the hidden self-doubts characteristic of male-type depression, this was absolutely unbearable to him.

These words, and the way she looked at him, broke his mirror big time. But this wouldn't even be so bad if it served as a wake-up call or helped get some valuable message across. It didn't. It just made him feel secretly ashamed and outwardly defensive and counterattacking. He didn't open up, but rather shut down.

One more example from a friend of mine helps illuminate this pattern:

I came out of the bathroom after shaving and I had nicked myself a little on the cheek. My girlfriend looked up at me and said "What happened to you? That's the second time you've done that this week." And I just went off. I started yelling at her, and then I stormed off, and our plans for the day were ruined. And it was all because of this broken-mirror thing. It was like she was really saying to me, "What kind of a loser are you that you can't do a basic guy-thing like shaving yourself?" I had a manhood attack. I know she didn't mean anything like that, but that's what I heard.

Perhaps the most important thing to understand about the broken-mirror process is the way in which we can misread the feelings we have. Your husband or boyfriend may feel hurt, and then confuse this with ascribing intention to you as if you meant to hurt him. Sometimes, in some relationships, that might actually be true. But for most of you, it's not. And he may have developed a dark view of you because he feels bad inside. That's the depression talking. The more depressed he is, the more susceptible he is to perceiving a world full of broken mirrors. You may do everything "right" (or at least be well-intentioned), and he still may have a broken-mirror experience. Like everything else you will learn from this book, there are no guarantees. You just want to figure out a way to increase the likelihood of success and of bringing out the best qualities in this man you love.

RECOGNIZING AND RESPONDING TO HIS DOWNERS

Troublesome conversations with a depressed man often start with a hook, and the hooks that we are focusing on in this chapter are known as *downers*. These are comments that are meant to provoke you in some way. They stir you up and can lead you to get drawn into a conversation that you will eventually regret. They are unconsciously (and I emphasize: *un*consciously) designed to draw you into the dark netherworld of depression so your partner doesn't feel so damned lonely in there. Depression loves company. You hear these comments, and you react to them. This makes perfect sense, because almost anyone hearing some of these provocative hooks would become worried, frustrated, or upset.

The game that is accidentally being played out here is "I'm hurting, but nothing you can say or do is going to help." In these situations, the instructions are clear: stop trying to help so much. It's not working. This game doesn't work if only one person plays.

You may not be able to control what your partner says and does, but you definitely can control whether you take the bait. You don't have to react the old way that hasn't been very helpful. And your capacity to not go there will not only help you feel better about yourself—it will also reduce the tensions in your relationship and the likelihood that your partner will keep repeating this verbal sparring pattern.

You need a different, more tuned-in response than the one your old instincts tell you to go with. Your master goals—always—are to take care of yourself, to be respectful of your partner, and to preserve the best aspects of your relationship. And modulating your responses can go a long way toward meeting these goals.

Tune In to Downers

Following are some responses you are probably tempted to come back with when you hear some of your partner's downers. And, unless you are a total saint, you have definitely said these things or things similar. But after these examples come specific suggestions for what to say instead. It's not that the "Unattuned" responses are actually untrue or unfair—they're just not helpful. And if your main goal is to truly be helpful (to yourself, to him, and to the relationship), then the "Tuned-in" items have a greater likelihood of getting the job done.

He says: It feels like you don't really care about *me*.

Unattuned: What else am I supposed to do? The problem is that you're too needy, not that I don't care!

Tuned-in: I'm really sorry it feels that way to you. I *do* care about you. Is there something I can do to make sure you know that?

He says: My life is going nowhere.

Unattuned: I can't believe you are saying that. Don't you realize how much you have to live for?

Tuned-in: You must feel so low to even be thinking these things, and I can only guess at how bad that is. But just remember that you've felt this way before, and it passes. We'll get through this together.

Recognizing and Responding to His Nervous-Makers

Depressed men also often make statements that make you feel nervous. These serve as hooks much like the downers do, because they trigger a wave of anxiety in you that you feel compelled to respond to. These generally occur when he is in an uncentered mood and more likely to propose reckless and "nervous-making" ideas.

He says: I feel like everybody's talking about me at work.

Unattuned: What are you talking about? You're always imagining things!

Tuned-in: God, I would hate feeling like that. What's happened that makes it seem that way to you?

He says: I can't believe how little I need to eat and sleep these days!

Unattuned: You're going to start acting crazy again!

Tuned-in:	I get nervous when you start feeling this way. We both know how out of control things can get, and we've seen these signs before. I'd really like you to call your doctor right away and tell him about this—for all our sakes. I love you—remember that.
He says:	I've worked really hard, and I really deserve to buy this boat.
Unattuned:	What are you talking about? We don't have the money for that and you know it!
Tuned-in:	We both know you've worked really hard, and I appreciate it. Let's sit down together and look over our finances and figure out if we can pull this off. Buying a boat would be great—but maybe there are other ways to feel better about our life together that will work better. Let's think about it.
He says:	Don't worry, honey—this next investment is going to make us back all the money we lost on the last one. It's a sure thing!
Unattuned:	Are you out of your mind? We almost went bankrupt with the last "sure thing"!
Tuned-in:	I'm glad you're so excited and confident about this. And I know you like to move quickly when you have a deal going. But I want us to sit down together and make a decision as a team on this one.

ACTIVE LISTENING

Many of you may already be familiar with the approach of responding to your partner's messages by using active listening. Some of you have learned the technique elsewhere, and others just know how to do it naturally. But, to be sure that you remember to use what you may already know, here are some of the basic principles of active listening that come in especially handy when dealing with communications from the depressed man in your life.

Active listening is a communication technique that encourages the other person to continue speaking. It also enables you to be as crystal clear as possible about what the other person is really saying. It's a way of checking in. It's called "active" listening because you not only listen but also *actively* let the other person know that you have really heard him.

Paraphrasing

Paraphrasing is stating in your own words what the other person is probably feeling.

- ■ "You sound really ___*(feeling)*___ about ___(situation)___ ."

- ■ "You must really feel ___*(feeling)*___ ."

- ■ "What I hear you saying is _____ ."

Clarifying

Clarifying involves asking questions to get more information, which helps you hear more specifics about the situation and feelings. Clarifying also lets the other person know you are interested in what he or she is saying.

- ■ "So, tell me what happened that got you so upset."

- ■ "How did you feel when that happened?"

Personalizing

Personalizing involves offering a personal example of feeling the same thing or being in the same situation.

- ■ "I think I know what you mean. I've been there too."

- ■ "I felt the same way when I lost my job. I think everyone does."

Personalizing helps the other person feel less alone, and it implies that someone else has experienced this and recovered from it. But be careful—personalizing can be harmful if you talk *too* much about yourself and steal the spotlight from the person who needs it.

■   "You think that was bad? Listen to what happened to me!"

Active listening does *not* mean cheering him up, defending yourself, trying to talk him out of his feelings, or just repeating back exactly what was said. There is a time and place for all of these responses, but they do not constitute active listening and aren't likely to help draw out his open expression of feelings.

Here are some examples that are *not* active listening and can be unhelpful:

DEFENDING YOURSELF

He says: I'm the only one who ever cleans up around here!

You say: You don't know half of the things I do!

TAKING CARE OF HIM

He says: You can't trust anyone around this place!

You say: Now, now, it's okay. It's all going to be better—I'll take care of it for you.

TALKING HIM OUT OF IT

He says: I'm really worried that my family is going to be mad at me for dropping out of school.

You say: You shouldn't feel that way.

PARROTING

He says: This place is really disgusting.

You say: It sounds like you think this place is really disgusting.

POSITIVE REINFORCEMENT

It is very tempting, when you have been dissatisfied with your partner's behavior for a long time, to continue to be critical and skeptical even when you start to see some changes in the desired direction. I call this "pulling the rug out," and admit that it may feel appropriate in the moment. Why shouldn't you be skeptical? After all, he has been withdrawing from you and the kids at night and on weekends for months or even years. Why should you start doing cartwheels just because he plans one family picnic?

These reactions are understandable but unproductive and dysfunctional. They won't help you. A more useful strategy is to use the psychological principle of *successive approximations*, in which the person receives reward or reinforcement for even moving slightly in the direction of the ultimate desired behavior. This principle applies to monkeys, pigeons, and kids—and to us adults, too. If you think of this technique as manipulation, don't. Reinforcing successive approximations simply means that you are fundamentally committed to bringing out the best in your partner and you are doing everything you can possibly do to increase the likelihood of achieving this result. He is not being controlled or manipulated. He is just getting the benefit of feeling good for doing the right thing for his relationship. It's only manipulation (in the negative sense) if you are exploiting him or trying to take advantage of him, and I'm operating on the assumption that this is not the case in your relationship.

The most powerful long-term combination for all behavior modification programs is reinforcing the positive and ignoring the negative. The impact of "catching him doing something right" is powerful. If you want to help bring your partner out of his depressive behavior patterns, always find a positive behavior to reinforce—even if it is only a period of time that has gone by without the presence of the negative. When you spend an hour shopping at the mall and he doesn't complain or act cynical, you may want to tell him that you love shopping with him when he is in this more positive mood. Note the times when you can tell he is tempted to act badly in a relationship but instead finds a different way. Note it to yourself, and make sure to let him know that you appreciate it.

Here's what my client Amy said about this:

Whenever I tell Paul about something I'm worried about, he tries to correct me. He tells me I wouldn't be feeling this way if I didn't take on so many projects. I hate that. I just want to complain, and I get to the point where I don't even want to let him know anything anymore because his reaction is so off base from what I need. He especially does this when he's depressed, I think, because he can't handle seeing me unhappy. He has to try and fix me because I bring him down.

I told him this recently, and I told him what I wanted from him instead. His feelings were hurt, but he took it okay. Then last week I told him I was having trouble sleeping. He was just very nice and tried to comfort me. No solutions or corrections. And I told him later that this was exactly what I needed from him. He beamed.

He's still not exactly the perfect communicator. But I want to let him know when he's doing it right.

EXERCISE: Don't Pull the Rug Out

The following is a list of situations that you might recognize. Listed first is the change that the man is demonstrating. Then comes the woman's discounting self-talk—followed by her response of pulling the rug out.

Get out your journal. After reading through the first three examples, write down in your journal the possible responses for the next one. Then write down a few of your own situations, and make notes of what would be more constructive self-talk for you in each one—followed by an example of a more rewarding and positive response.

1. *His behavior:* Upon your request, he has made an effort to demonstrate more affection and appreciation toward you.
   Your discounting self-talk: "He never would have done this on his own."
   Pulling the rug out: "Yes, you've been showing more affection and appreciation lately, but it's just because the counselor told you to. You don't really mean it."

   Instead, try this:

Constructive self-talk: "I can tell he's trying. This is more of what I need from him."
Rewarding response: "It feels great to me that you've been touching me more. It's starting to feel like the old days."

2. *His behavior:* Upon your request, he has made an effort to socialize more with your family when they come over to visit.
    Your discounting self-talk: "I don't think I can forgive him for letting me down so much in the past."
    Pulling the rug out: "Why do you even bother? I know you don't want to be here with them, and so do they!"

    Instead, try this:

    Constructive self-talk: "I like seeing some of his new behaviors, and I can't let myself stay stuck in the past."
    Rewarding response: "It really means a lot to me that you've been trying so hard with my family."

3. *His behavior:* Upon your request, he has been helping out more with the kids at night.
    Your discounting self-talk: "What good is it to me if he doesn't do it the way I think it should be done?"
    Pulling the rug out: "I know you've been giving the kids baths more often, but you're not doing it right."

    Instead, try this:

    Constructive self-talk: "This is really new for him to help out more."
    Rewarding response: "I love it that you've been taking over the kids' baths. Can I give you a few tips about what I've found that works well?"

4. *His behavior:* Upon your request, he has made an effort to be less self-involved and listen more to what you are going through.
    Your discounting self-talk: "If I don't stay on his case about making these changes, he's just going to get complacent. I can't let up."

Pulling the rug out: "Of course you're listening to me talk more about my feelings now, but that's only because I'm watching you so carefully. As soon as I take the pressure off, this will all go back to the way it used to be."

Instead, try this:

Constructive self-talk:

Rewarding response:

SUMMARY

When you understand the power of the broken-mirror phenomenon in a depressed man's psychological life, you are likely to recognize many examples where you've inadvertently said or done something that has driven him further into his shell. Sometimes this can't be helped—but many times it can. If you follow basic communication principles and don't let yourself get drawn in to your partner's downer comments, your response can be more tuned-in to what he needs from you emotionally. It is especially important to recognize the value of rewarding successive approximations. The more you know about how to do this, the more likely that you will have a long-term positive influence on your partner's behavior.

CHAPTER 5

You Are Not a
Punching Bag: Enabling

In the preceding chapter, you learned about the best ways to support your depressed partner and how to be especially attuned to the pain he is going through. In this chapter, you will learn about how to balance that support and understanding with the equally important challenge of taking care of yourself and setting limits.

You want to support the man in your life—without crossing over the toxic line into being an enabler or codependent. Anyone who has read a magazine in the past fifteen years has at least some idea of what *codependency* or *enabling* are. They both mean that you *excessively* put the needs of another person ahead of your own. The key word here is "excessively," because many behaviors that are often labeled as codependent or examples of enabling are actually just supportive, generous, and loving.

Understanding the difference between acts of loving kindness and acts of enabling is best reflected in the well-known Serenity Prayer: "God grant me the serenity to accept the things I cannot change, courage to change the things I can, and the wisdom to know the difference." You want to develop the wisdom to know the difference.

The research about codependency and enabling originally emerged from the field of family dynamics and alcoholism, and it brought to light the ways in which family members covered up for the alcoholic person. The kids would want to make sure to not get Mom upset, or she might start drinking. The wife would call in to her husband's workplace and report that he had the flu, when he was actually nursing a nasty hangover.

Now the concept is applied to any situation in which one person in a relationship excessively suspends his or her own needs and engages in behaviors that contribute to a massive cover-up of another person's problem. And, in this discussion, I'm applying these ideas to the ways in which you, as the wife or partner of a depressed man, may be giving up and covering up too much—in ways that help neither you, nor him, nor your relationship.

EXERCISE: Enabling Your Depressed Partner

To get some idea of whether or not you are engaging in patterns of enabling, ask yourself the following questions. Answer them and write down any accompanying thoughts in your journal. Any of these patterns are troublesome; three or more give a serious indication that you are engaging in classic codependent behavior. Be careful in these assessments, however—remember that not all worrying or caretaking is codependent. (Any of you who are parents, for instance, will certainly know what it's like to worry about someone else's mood and emotional state more than your own!)

1. Do you think more about his behavior and problems than about your own life?

2. Do you feel anxious about his moods and constantly wait for the next storm to hit?

3. Do you judge the state of your relationship by what kind of mood he seems to be in?

4. Do you worry that he will fall apart if you stop trying to manage his behavior?

5. Do you blame yourself for his moods and unhappiness?

6. Do you cover up for him when he doesn't go in to work or withdraws from commitments?

7. Do you catch yourself denying that he has any problems and become angry or defensive when others suggest there is something wrong with him?

STRATEGIES TO STOP ENABLING

1. Remember that you did not cause his problems.

2. Remember that you can't control what he thinks, feels, or does.

3. Remember that you can't fix him.

4. Don't make excuses or cover up for his bad moods or bad behavior.

5. Admit to yourself he has a real problem that may need professional help.

6. As best as possible, do not allow his moods to interrupt your normal family routines.

7. Set limits on what you will and won't do. Be firm and stick to these limits. It's natural to want to take care of those you love, but in some cases, it doesn't help.

8. Do whatever you can to distract yourself from some of the worry and distress that you feel in relation to your partner. Talk to your friends. Make sure you have interesting activities. Take care of yourself physically and spiritually.

9. Protect yourself and your children at all costs. If you or your children are being significantly damaged by his moods or behaviors, you must find a way to intervene or leave.

WHEN HE IS ANGRY AND BLAMING

In learning to take care of yourself in a relationship with a depressed (and often angry and blaming) man, it is essential to identify the pattern of *blaming* hooks. Like the ways in which the downers and the nervous-makers from the previous chapter can hook you, responding to these hooks often brings out a side of you that isn't pretty and that you do not like. Later you wonder how you ended up getting into an argument like you did. You hear things coming out of your mouth that you vowed never to say, and you hate yourself for it. For those of you with kids (particularly teenagers), you will easily recognize this pattern. Except that this time your reaction isn't "I can't believe I said these things to my kids—like my mother did" but rather "I can't believe I said these things to my husband—like my mother did."

Again, remember that you are always trying to find the right balance between doing too much caretaking (enabling, codependency, or passivity) and responding with too much retaliation, hostility, and defensiveness. This middle ground, easy to describe and quite difficult to consistently locate, is otherwise known as assertiveness: taking care of your needs, thoughts, and feelings in a way that is least likely to create anger or defensiveness in the other person.

EXERCISE: Responding to Anger and Blame

Here are some guidelines for the best responses to anger and blame statements:

1. Calmly clarify how you feel about what he has said.

2. Use as little counter-blame or character assassination as possible.

3. Acknowledge whatever truth there may be in his accusation, but insist that he keep it in perspective and stop excessive blame.

4. Be polite and respectful.

5. Be firm and clear in what you do not agree with or will not tolerate.

6. Make "I" statements like "I feel worried" rather than "you" statements like "You're being stupid."

7. Ask questions to get him to clarify specifically what he is upset about.

8. Offer reassurance about your love and belief in him whenever humanly possible.

Below is a list of *blamers*. These are typical statements that emerge from male-type depression guys when they are in a bad mood. Some of the examples below include suggested responses from you. For the last two examples, write down in your journal what you might say in your own language that follows these principles. Then add a few more examples of the provocative statements your partner has at times made to you, and design a response that you would like to use in the future.

■ "Why do you always want to ruin my fun?"

Best response: "I'm sorry you feel that I try to ruin your fun—I don't think I do. Have I just done something that's bothering you?"

■ "I have plenty of money and it's none of your business what I buy. Don't you want me to enjoy something for once?"

Best response: "Of course I want you to enjoy things. I love you. But this is our money together, and we need to figure out a way to make these decisions together."

■ "You never want to do anything with me."

Best response: "Please be careful with the 'always' and 'nevers.' It really upsets when me when you do that."

■ "Don't you get it? The reason I go to all these porn sites is because you're never interested in sex!"

Best response: "I know you're frustrated with our sex life, and we're both working on it. But your decision to check out all the porn sites is your decision alone, and I am not responsible for it."

- "You've got to be kidding! Me—depressed? You're the one who's depressed!"

Best response: "I saw you talking with that boyfriend of yours from work!"

■

Best response:

SETTING CLEAR LIMITS

Women often end up caught between a rock and a hard place with men who are depressed, emotionally sensitive, and easily shamed. On the one hand, you want to be careful not to confront him too much because you are understandably worried that he will hear the message as "You are depressed and dysfunctional and you need some pills to get your sorry life together!" On the other hand, you don't want to be an enabler. You don't want to pretend that the emperor is wearing clothes when he is actually naked and falling apart. But when you confront him, you risk being the "bitch." And when you back off and don't say anything, you can feel like an enabler.

To complicate these issues further, many men (consciously or unconsciously) have maneuvered the relationship into a configuration in which you have learned that it's not in your best interest to wake the sleeping giant. He will attack you for your timing, for your relentlessness, for your tone of voice, for your "need to control" him. And the ultimate trump card is either overtly expressed or waits in the wings: "You are such a bitch!"

Behavior

Sometimes "tough love" is the most generous kind of love of all. Not only is it often an act of self-preservation for you to disengage from enabling behaviors—it can also be a genuine check and balance on your depressed partner's behavior and perceptions.

When your partner's behavior is destructive to him, to you, and to the family, you have an obligation to set limits. One client of mine, Kristi, watched for months as her husband, Andrew, sunk deeper and deeper into his depression. She watched as he felt bad, blamed her, blew up at the kids, became emotionally clingy and possessive with her, withdrew from other people, and started failing at his job. They tried couples therapy to work out the marital problems, but he couldn't let go of his relentless blame of her.

For many of the reasons that men feel threatened by the word, Andrew would not accept the label of depression. So Kristi finally summoned up the courage to tell it like it is and set a limit:

> Andrew, you may not be willing to see it or admit it, but you are depressed. I see it, the kids see it. Our therapist really sees it. I can't do this anymore. You either need to go on antidepressants, or we are separating. I love you—but now it's up to you.

Andrew spewed and sputtered and resisted. But he started anti-depressants, so Kristi hung in there with him. And four weeks later, after the antidepressants had kicked in, he told Kristi: "I can't believe what I was thinking and what I was doing back then!"

Mind Games

Not only is it important to set limits on behaviors that directly impact you or your family, but you'll also want to be able to recognize and short-circuit some of your partner's more subtle mind games.

Rosa was an eighteen-year-old girl whose boyfriend had jumped off a bridge and killed himself the previous year when she rejected him. Rosa's father, Rory, had a long history of agitated, blaming, male-type depression patterns. On this occasion, about a year after the suicide, Rosa and Rory were arguing in the car. She was hounding him about always trying to get his way. They bickered and squabbled. Finally he pulled over dramatically and jerked the car to a stop. He opened the door, started crawling out, and boldly announced, "Maybe I'll just go shoot myself!"

"Maybe I'll just go shoot myself"? This, spoken to a girl whose boyfriend took his own life by jumping off a bridge only a year before, tearing an irreparable hole in her heart and her psyche. Rosa, stunned, could do nothing but sit and stare into space and start to cry.

Rory may not have been able to acknowledge this consciously, but he engaged in a classic mind game played by a depressed person in blaming mode. When Rory threatened suicide, he was operating out of pure defensiveness. "I can't handle what you are telling me, and I can't think of any other way to get you to shut up!" The desperation of depression leads people to say and do things that they normally wouldn't, because they have entered the survival zone based on perceived emotional threat.

The appropriate response from Rosa, or from you if your husband or boyfriend says something like this, is, "I don't care how upset you are, or how depressed you are, or how mad you are at me—don't you *ever* say anything like that to me again!"

USING NONTHREATENING MESSAGES

When you set the kinds of limits that you believe are really necessary, you want to be as straightforward and unequivocal as possible—and you need to be effective. So, in addition to being clear, you also need to do everything in your power to decrease the likelihood of creating a defensive reaction from your partner. This is not always possible, but it's worth your effort to do everything possible to succeed at your ultimate goal: taking care of yourself and getting through to him.

There are important principles to keep in mind about reducing the threat level of the messages you send. The broken-mirror principles, reviewed in chapter 4, will help you stay on track. Criticisms or complaints will often be perceived by depressed men as much more condemning messages than they were intended. While, ultimately, it is his responsibility to find a way to tolerate this, it is your responsibility to not break any more mirrors than you have to.

Beware of Emotional Hijacking

Another way of understanding how important it is to anticipate the reactions of your depressed partner emerges from recent research in the field of neurochemistry.

The *amygdala*, a tiny almond-shaped structure in the primitive limbic system, is at the center of the brain's emotional life. The amygdala functions a lot like a security alarm you might have in your home. When it reads some event as violating the known rules of safe behavior, it goes nuts and sets off a mental alarm, effectively putting us in a zone where we can't really think straight. Situations that your brain perceives as emotional emergencies stimulate signals to the amygdala. The amygdala then scans the information for potential danger. The amygdala is very dependent on associational patterns; if something about the current event is similar to an emotionally charged memory from the past, the limbic system is likely to be activated in full force.

So when your partner perceives something you are doing or saying as a message that telegraphs "She doesn't love me," "She is disrespecting me," or "She might be leaving me," signals are activated along a pathway that serves as an express route to the amygdala. Once your partner's brain determines that a situation represents a threat, a state of "national emergency" is declared. The amygdala lights up the entire brain and body before the neocortex ever gets into the act. The neocortex, switchboard for all of our most advanced functions and cognitive capacities, is bypassed. In other words, your partner's brain is emotionally hijacked by his limbic system.

In our modern age, we have developed (for better or worse) the capacity to perceive threat not only from the saber-toothed tiger outside of our cave or the suspicious-looking guy in the parking lot. We also react to symbolic threats to our self-esteem. We are threatened by being dissed. And nowhere are we all (and especially someone who is depressed, with easily activated depressing narratives) more vulnerable than in our most emotionally intimate relationships.

Maybe it shouldn't be this way, and maybe it feels unfair if you are in a relationship with a man who is easily emotionally hijacked. But that's just the way it is. And it's in everybody's best interest to find ways to minimize the likelihood of bringing up threatening narratives, broken mirrors, and emotional hijacking. You would expect no less from him.

EXERCISE: Asking for Change

One method to use when you want to communicate your feelings, meanings, and intentions in the most direct and respectful way possible is by using the "Asking for Change" model. The use of I messages in this approach is specific, nonjudgmental, and focused on the speaker. In contrast, you messages are often received as hostile, blaming, and focused on the other person. Reframing you messages into I messages with very specific behavioral information can help you communicate, because your partner is less likely to feel attacked.

After you read these examples, get out your journal and write down three examples of your own. I recommend telling your partner that you are trying this out, then using this approach and getting feedback from him about how it came across.

Construct I messages by using these four phrases:

1. **When you** (state the behavior).

2. **I feel** (state the feeling) **because** (explain in more detail). Note: Using the word "because" with an explanation can help by giving the other person more information to understand you.

3. **I wish** (state what you would prefer instead).

4. **And if you can do that, I will** (explain how the other person will benefit).

The different parts of the I message do not have to be delivered in exact order. The important thing is to keep the focus on yourself and to stay away from blame. Here are some examples:

- **When you** take long phone calls during dinner, **I get angry** because I begin to think you don't want to talk to me. **I wish** you would tell whoever's calling that you'll call back because we're in the middle of dinner. And **if you can do that, I'll** make sure not to hassle you so much about being on the phone later.

- **When you** don't come home on time or call, **I get worried** that something has happened to you. **I would really like** you to call me if you're gong to be late. **And if you can do that, I promise** not to have an attitude when you get home.

Now write in your journal three examples from your life.

Direct Threat Reducers

Through their words, body language, tone of voice, and subtle behaviors, the most successful couples communicate a fundamental message of acceptance, saying in effect, "Please don't worry—I really like you, and I really love you." Once that basic message is established, they can afford to move on to the issue at hand, "I don't like this specific behavior, and I'd like you to change it." For the most part, the partner can handle this because it is not perceived as a fundamental threat. The limbic system is not activated; the fundamental sense of appreciation serves as an antithreat device.

One of the most potent provocations for many of us, and especially for men suffering from male-type depression who are quick to assume the worst, is what Gottman refers to as a "negative start-up" (1999). The negative start-up from you to your husband or boyfriend might be something like, "How come you never clean up anything around here?" You are upset because it feels like the distribution of labor at home is not fair. And the message has a hostile tone, accuses him of overall laziness and sloth, describes his behavior in global negative terms—and in fact is not even a question at all. It is pure put-down and is likely to be met with a defensive or overtly hostile response.

The "softened start-up" sounds something like, "Hey, I'm really feeling overloaded with the state of the house. Can we sit down and figure out a plan so we can get it cleaned up?" This includes an I message, makes no accusations, is very specific about the problem, and offers a team approach to solving it. No guarantees, but this is much more likely to generate a positive response. Unless your partner is extremely sensitive and/or in a very bad mood, he is not likely to perceive this as an attack on his manhood.

Indirect Threat Reducers

Another set of behaviors that help reduce the perception of threat when you are offering criticism or complaints is much more indirect, but just as meaningful and powerful. These behavior patterns, which every successful couple employs at one time or another, all have the effect of softening a potential blow and lightening up the atmosphere. Some couples seem to know how to do these naturally, but we can all benefit from being more conscious of what works.

The first category is called the "I still love you" strategies. All of these communicate, without direct words, "No matter how much we are arguing right now, not to worry. I still love you!"

- **Using physical affection:** Touch your partner in a loving way when you are trying to get something across to him (message: "I love you"). For example, stroking his arm or rubbing his back can work wonders.

- **The cup of coffee:** In the middle of a tense/defensive discussion, get up to pour yourself a cup of coffee or get a cookie, bringing one to him as well (message: "I really care about you").

- **"Isn't she cute?":** Focus on something cute about the baby or the new backyard patio in the middle of a sensitive discussion (message: "We have so much good stuff in our lives together").

- **Self-deprecating humor:** Make a gentle joke about yourself when making requests. For example, when trying to get your partner to clean up his clutter more you could say, "I know I'm not exactly Martha Stewart when it comes to keeping our house clean, but . . . (message: "We're in this together").

The second category I describe simply as "not making a bad moment even worse." It requires you to consciously choose to ignore certain potentially irritating or provocative behaviors from your depressed partner. We all do this—or at least anyone in a reasonably successful relationship does this. You shouldn't ignore the big ones or the relentless ones; that is enabling. But you can ignore or redirect the minor ones; that's just smart.

- **Staying in the present.** You approach him with something that needs to be discussed. He gets defensive and starts bringing up your faults. Just stay calm, patient, and focused. Tempting as it might be, don't bring up issues from the past or get into discussions about other complaints. Just remind him of the subject at hand.

■ **Forfeiting the last word.** Some people (actually, many people) insist on getting the last word in an argument. When both of you insist on the last word, the argument can seem endless. When one person manages to let the last-word opportunity go by, the game is usually over.

Example: The two of you are arguing. You tell him he is being selfish. He walks away and calls out, "Who was being selfish last night when you got to watch your movie?" You choose not to respond. He gets the last word. So what?

■ **Ignoring the negative.** Many of the instructions about staying connected with or getting through to a depressed man involve the Herculean task of ignoring the negative. Remember that you have a mission, which is to get the communication process going, and his subterfuge is just flak that doesn't need to stop you or provoke you into a counterattack.

Example: He sits down at the dinner table in a bad mood. He tells you that there's something wrong with the chicken and that it must be overcooked. You decide not to respond to his ungrateful attitude and just let him be moody. Moods often pass if the other person doesn't react or make it worse.

■ **Allowing space.** When your partner has become defensive and won't let you in, sometimes the most effective strategy is a very old-fashioned one: just back off and give him some space. Many couples have mastered the art of stepping aside and waiting for the storm to pass. This does not qualify as a problem-solving technique, nor does it extend a path toward exploring the deeper feelings and issues that triggered the conflict in the first place. But used occasionally, this strategy can ease tension in your relationship.

Example: You have complained to your boyfriend that he has been drinking too much at parties and it's really starting to bother you. He says, "That is such crap. I can't even talk to you at all!" You wait. You do not go after him to try to drill home the point. You let him have some space to chew on the issue and digest it without being forced to get defensive.

INSISTING ON TWINSHIP

If I were writing a bill of rights for partners of the depressed, I'd include the following right: The partner of the depressed man is entitled to insist on twinship and the team approach.

Twinship is a term borrowed from the field of self psychology (Shapiro 1995) that I usually define as offering the individual increased self-cohesion through an identification with others—a sense of being like others, in the same "club" or "clan." In other words, we all have a very strong need to feel like we share fundamental experiences and qualities with the people we have chosen in our lives. The way this applies to your relationship with a depressed man is that you have every right to insist that he share responsibility for the problems in the relationship and not just blame his unhappiness on you. You can also expect him to share responsibility for taking charge of these problems. It is totally within your rights—in fact, I would insist that it is in everybody's best interest—for you to require certain basic behaviors and participation from your partner in exchange for committing yourself to helping him with his problems and working on the relationship.

The next exercise is a sample contract of what you can reasonably and fairly offer to your depressed partner. You can promise him a lot—if you know he is trying and taking this process seriously. But if you're the only one promising, you are enabling. If you promise nothing and simply insist that he change, you are being withholding. If you contract to work on this together, you are initiating the deeply healing process of twinship.

(The exception to this rule applies when anyone in a relationship is behaving in a truly abusive fashion: physical abuse, extreme verbal abuse, infidelity, substance abuse, etc. In these situations, it would be inappropriate to promise anything in response to behavioral changes. The only thing to offer is recognition, for instance, "I'm glad you have stopped yelling at me in front of the kids.")

Use the items in this exercise as a sample. In your journal, pick out the items here that work for you, take out the ones that don't, and add your own. Review these with your partner if you feel like he will be receptive to the conversation.

EXERCISE: My Commitment to You

I'm willing to do whatever I can to communicate respectfully to you so that you know that I love you and care about you.

I am willing to offer criticisms, feedback, or requests about your specific behavior only, without putting you down or indicting your whole personality.

I'm willing to learn new techniques to help you get through this—if you are too.

I understand your depression is an illness, and I'm willing to work with you instead of blaming you—if I know that you are trying.

Within reason, I am willing to make changes in my own lifestyle to help us get through this successfully (drinking patterns, patterns of social involvement and entertaining, exercising together, etc.), as long as I see you committed to your own changes as well.

I know helping you with this may cost us a lot in time, money, and energy, but it's 100 percent worth it to save our relationship.

I am committed to you and to this relationship, and I'm willing to try what the therapists and books are suggesting we try to do for _____ months. If you have not been able to make a lot of the changes that I need from you by then, then I will have to reconsider whether I can stay in this relationship.

_____

Your Name   Date

_____

Your Partner's Name   Date

SUMMARY

Although you are trying to find ways to respect and get through to the depressed man in your life, you also need to beware of becoming an enabler. It is your job—for yourself, for him, and for the relationship—to set reasonable limits about what you will tolerate and what you won't. You have a right to set limits on his angry or blaming comments, his destructive behavior, and on his mind games. There are ways to increase the likelihood of these limits coming across as loving and reasonable rather than as assaults. You also have a reasonable right to twinship and a team approach to working on these problems.

CHAPTER 6

Helping Him with Treatment: Psychological

Now that you know more about male depression and about the different ways that you can be both understanding and limit-setting, it is also important to know about all the different treatment strategies for depression—and how you can encourage your partner to utilize them.

Although this book isn't a treatment manual for depressed men, it is a guide for the people who are in relationships with them. It is in your best interest to be as knowledgeable as possible about the variety of available antidepressant strategies: psychological, biological, and behavioral. You can be a valuable resource for your partner if you can recommend different therapies, one or more of which might hit the mark for him. Between this chapter and the next one, you will develop at least a basic knowledge of the most important interventions.

Throughout this chapter, you will learn about what we currently know about alleviating depression, and especially male-type depression, without medication or strategies that involve the physical (nutrition, alternative medicine, etc.). The biological and medical interventions are in the next chapter, and what we know about psychological, behavioral, and interpersonal interventions are in this chapter.

HELPING HIM REMEMBER WHAT HE ALREADY KNOWS

A great teacher of mine, famed psychiatrist Milton Erickson, used to say, "There are so many things you know how to do, it's just that you haven't always known that you know them." While we all know that people suffering from depression can benefit from new interventions that they have never tried before, one of the guiding principles in helping people cope involves helping them remember how they have been successful in the past. Success here may simply mean that they recall times in the past when they survived a depressive episode or maintained a reasonably positive attitude in the face of difficult circumstances. It may mean times when they felt sluggish or lethargic and started exercising more. Or it could be times when they told someone else how they were feeling and ended up feeling unburdened and less lonely.

When planning any kind of treatment or intervention, the first question I always ask a depressed man is "How have you been successful with managing your depression in the past?" The answer to that question, often quite idiosyncratic, leads to the conclusion that many of the skills necessary to pull out of his low moods already exist as part of his behavioral repertoire. It's just that he has forgotten them, or that the weight of some emotional burden, stress, or biochemical breakdown has temporarily blocked his access to the warehouse of information that predates this current state.

Remember that there are many things you know how to do, it's just that you haven't always known that you know them. Remind him of this whenever you can. Remind him of what you have always loved about him and how he has been successful on so many levels at so many different times in his life.

BASIC STRATEGIES

In the exercise below is a list of basic guidelines that a depressed man should keep in mind as he tries to find a way out of the depressed mood and depressive behaviors. All of these will be explained in more detail throughout this chapter.

EXERCISE: Strategies for Managing Depression

In your journal, make note of the strategies below that you think you could suggest to the depressed man in your life, ones that he might be reasonably receptive to. Try bringing these up to him in language that is comfortable to you and that you guess will be comfortable to him.

For example, you may just decide to show him this list and go over it together. Or you may want to encourage him to exercise by saying, "It would be really fun if we worked out (went swimming, played volleyball, went for a walk, etc.) together. Want to join me?" If he is feeling overwhelmed by the prospect of accomplishing a task like cleaning out the garage, you could suggest this: "Let's just carve it up into small chunks. Saturday, let's just go through and clear out the old stuff we don't need. We can do that in an hour. Then next weekend, we'll take an hour to go through the small tools and boxes of screws and get them organized. If we put in an hour every weekend, it'll be done in six weeks without a whole lot of pain."

STRATEGIES

- He needs to get some exercise! For a thousand reasons, this is one of the most potent interventions for depression.

- He can benefit from discovering, or rediscovering, any activities or relationships that offer him a sense of meaning and fulfillment. He may have to think about this more carefully than he usually does and push himself to engage in them even when he doesn't feel like it.

- He needs to keep his goals realistic and expect his mood to improve gradually, not immediately. Any improvement should be celebrated. One day at a time!

- It can really help him to find someone—his kids, somebody else's kids, employees, homeless people at soup kitchens, friends—to whom he can offer something of himself. This is not only nice, it's also very selfish in the best sense of the word.

- He needs to break large tasks into small ones. There is nothing more discouraging than looking at a whole house that is a mess. He can think of it as one room at a time, or even one corner at a time.

- It is really helpful for him to try to be with other people and to confide in someone, and to let his family and friends help him.

- Anhedonia is his enemy; finding any activities or people that offer him some spark of pleasure will help.

- He should try not to make any major decision when he is in the thick of the depression—especially the ultimate permanent decision of taking his own life. Depressive moods play tricks with the brain and judgment cannot always be trusted under these circumstances.

- There is nothing more important than for him to keep track of—and challenge—his self-talk and the stories he tells about himself, his relationships, and the future.

- He needs to adopt the philosophy of "Fake it until you make it." Even if he doesn't feel like exercising, playing with his kids, or cleaning out his car, he should do it anyway. The more he acts like a nondepressed person, the more likely it is that he will become one.

THE POWER OF NEW STORIES

The stories that a man tells himself about his life and his relationships can either destroy or enhance his mood, symptoms, and behaviors. The narrative can easily intensify the avoidance, withdrawal, and acting out—or liberate the man to handle the challenge of depression in new and more successful ways.

The negative narratives are known as *depressiogenic thinking*: self-talk patterns that generate depression just like carcinogenic substances generate cancer (Seligman 1998).

What this really boils down to is helping men develop what Seligman describes as *flexible optimism* (1998). This is based on his studies clearly indicating that optimism is usually a more psychologically healthy perspective, but only in situations where it is based in reality. For the man who sees a job setback as resulting from some personal flaw ("I'm stupid"), thus feeling more depressed, treatment involves helping him develop a story based on something he can change ("If I developed better skills in that area, I'd be more valuable for my company.")

You can't change his stories. Only he can do that. But you can recognize how powerfully these stories govern his moods, attitudes, and behaviors. If you understand how these work, you can offer him some gentle feedback or influence at crucial moments to help him keep his stories in perspective (explained in the "What you can do" sections in the pages to follow).

The most widely researched and used clinical intervention for depression is known as *cognitive behavioral therapy*. This is a treatment approach based on the theory that how one thinks about issues in one's life will have a direct impact on mood, emotions, and ultimately behaviors. The treatment approach involves the dual strategy of targeting and challenging dysfunctional beliefs (also known as self-talk, cognitions, stories, or personal narratives) and encouraging new behaviors that are likely to lead to symptom relief and personal development.

What you can do. Encourage his therapy. Encourage him to read self-help books that emphasize cognitive behavioral approaches, like Burns's *The Feeling Good Handbook* (1999), Seligman's *Learned Optimism: How to Change Your Mind and Your Life* (1998), Yapko's *Breaking the Patterns of Depression* (1998), and McKay and Fanning's *Self-Esteem* (2000).

Evidence

Seligman identifies the four basic strategies by which someone can dispute the labels or stories that are plaguing him. The first strategy is evidence. The absolute most powerful intervention for a man to change negative, pessimistic, depressiogenic beliefs is to prove to himself that they are not accurate. Or at least not as comprehensively and morbidly accurate as he has come to believe.

What you can do. When you hear your partner saying that he feels left out in social situations, gently point out to him the situations in which this has not been true, when he has actually fit in just fine. Or if he is feeling discouraged about blowing up at the kids, remind him that least week your son said to you, "Daddy's not getting mad as much as he did before, is he?"

Alternatives

There are almost always multiple alternative narratives to describe a life situation. The more optimistic man has the capacity to focus on the changeable, the specific, and the nonpersonal: "I don't have to keep doing this. It has only happened in certain situations and not in others, and many of these times it has not been my fault (or at least there was plenty of responsibility to go around)." This leads to a conclusion that is not ridiculously rosy, but simply realistic: "It's not great, but not as bad as I thought."

What you can do. When your partner blames himself for not being successful enough in his job, acknowledge that he has made some mistakes in judgment—but gently point out to him that one job does not a career make. Or, when he looks in a mirror and says, "I'm really losing it, aren't I?" you can joke with him about how normal it is to get a little bulge at his age. It does not have to be a sign of personal weakness.

Implications

Seligman's third strategy focuses on implications. Even if this belief is correct, how bad is it really? What does it really suggest for the future? This challenge in self-talk requires the capacity to "decatastrophize" the story.

What you can do. Encourage him to think like this: "Okay, even if I did fail at this job, I still have a lot of other opportunities and skills.

This doesn't mean I am stupid or a failure." Whenever you can, remind him of all the positives in his life—including you. And always remind him that this tough period is temporary. You have both been through these before, and you will weather them again.

Usefulness

Usefulness is Seligman's fourth strategy. Even if a negative belief is true, get practical with it. Is it doing him any good to keep focusing on the belief? "Yes, it is probably true that I keep withdrawing in social situations whenever I feel like people are judging me. And it probably gets in my way in terms of people feeling comfortable with me or liking me. But what is the point of focusing on this? It just makes it worse—which is the last thing I need!"

What you can do. Point out to him that the regret he feels about being a distant or even abusive father when the kids were younger only has value if it motivates him to change. After that, it is simply paralyzing. And remind him that his most important values as a father will not be honored if he shuts himself down. If he is having trouble performing sexually, suggest that the two of you just spend time touching each other nonsexually in bed—because his worrying about performance is only making the situation worse.

From Blaming to Twinship

As we discussed earlier, one of the nastiest features of male depression is the pattern of blaming. This blaming pattern is in direct proportion to the man's lack of tolerance for experiencing negative emotions and identifying himself as weak or powerless. He blames others (and especially you) when things don't feel right instead of either blaming himself or simply recognizing that shit happens.

The twinship perspective is much more adaptive at this point. *Twinship* refers to the need we all have to be members of the same club or clan: the experience that "we are all in this together" or at least "neither of us is perfect."

Here's an insight about twinship from one of my male-type depression clients:

> My wife and I took off with our kids to the beach, and she forgot to bring the baby wipes. In the past, when I was depressed and everything irritated me, all I did was get mad at her and tell her how stupid she was. Now it looks different. Don't get me wrong—it's still irritating when she does something like that. But I forget things too. We're in this together. When I remember that, I can blow it off rather than blowing up.

Here, the two of you are profoundly alike. You are no longer the enemy, but rather a comrade along the difficult road of life who is also suffering, feeling deprived, worried, or not totally and completely fulfilled. When he thinks of his relationship with you as a twinship experience, he is less likely to feel resentful and victimized. And he is less likely to approach you in ways that will make you defensive!

What you can do. When he is blaming you or feeling sorry for himself, remind him that the two of you are in this together. It helps if you can deliver this message without sounding angry and defensive. If you can get through, you will be offering him a profoundly valuable antidepressant by helping him rewrite his depressiogenic narratives. Or, when he feels defeated by trying to get the kids to listen to him, remind him of how often you feel the exact same way.

Religion and Faith

Perhaps one of the most profound examples of how personal narrative can determine mood and coping skills is evident in the relationship between religious belief and depression. Studies have found that churchgoers, in general, experience less depression than nonchurchgoers (Brown and Harris 1978). Depressive and pessimistic men tend to see failure as something that is a lasting source of hopelessness. Churchgoers or not, people of faith often have the capacity to maintain a larger perspective. A belief in God and an afterlife often means that life setbacks are only temporary defeats. A person with faith can reframe them in that context: "Bad things that happen to me all have meaning. They provide lessons. They are all part of God's plan. In the afterlife, I will suffer no more. That which does not kill me makes me stronger." And Hindus or Buddhists may perceive suffering as an opportunity to deal with karma—with another chance to get it right in the next lifetime.

What you can do. Don't try to ram religion down his throat. But if the depressed man in your life is religious or is even open to thinking in spiritual or religious terms, it can be enormously comforting and inspiring to remind him that his setbacks and his faults are tremendous opportunities for growth and a renewal of faith. They may even be viewed as part of a divine plan for him, which strips them of the toxicity and allows them to be actually welcomed as gifts. You may find it helpful to remind him that God has a plan for him, and some of the rough times he is going through are all part of the plan.

DISTRACTION: THE ANTIDOTE TO RUMINATION

Ruminations are mantras. They circle around in our brains and loop again and again and again. They won't cut us any slack. Ruminations, actually, can be either positive or negative. But ruminators who are also pessimists are otherwise known as depressives. That particular combination, in fact, is especially potent. Even people who are pessimistic in their personal narratives can usually avoid the more oppressive levels of depression if they refrain from ruminating.

Wenzlaff reports that there is an automatic quality to the negative thinking of depressed people (1993). The negative thoughts are right out in front of them and easy to grab on to, interfering with the ability to focus elsewhere. In contrast, positive or more realistic self-talk fades into the background. Anyone who is depressed suffers from a particular deficit in the suppression of negative material.

Ruminators often convince themselves that they are doing some important work by thinking things through very carefully. This may be true for the first ten minutes, but not for the next few hours, days, or years. One example of ruminative thinking is that of the man who goes back and forth and back and forth about an important issue—and then makes an impulsive decision anyway. Changing either rumination or pessimism helps relieve depression. Changing both helps the most.

Distraction

Research (Tice and Baumeister 1993) and common sense are unified in recognizing the value of distraction as a way to allow the brain and nervous system to shift gears when a person is upset or depressed. In fact, in all mood management (including depression, anxiety, and anger), distraction emerges as a most potent mind-altering technique (Zillman 1993).

Simply put, rumination prolongs depressed mood, and successful distraction shortens it. Both depressed and nondepressed people report that one of the most common ways they attempt to cope with unwanted thoughts is to try to eliminate them by thinking of something else (Wenzlaff 1993).

However, just "thinking it over" is not always the ticket if a guy is depressed. Many men who just try to "take a break and think things over" are more than likely to use the time to ruminate about things that depress them rather than focus on something that is positive or at least neutral and distracting. Studies show that nondepressed people are able to let go of focusing on disturbing events over time (Wenzlaff 1993). Depressed people, however, actually become more and more obsessed with the bad events, even as they get further away in time from when they happened.

If distraction helps your partner pull out of the depths of a depressed mood or helps him manage his critical, blaming, and destructive interactions with you or the kids, then it's a brilliant and creative use of his personal resources, and you should encourage it. Obviously, if he consistently employs distraction and never comes around to face the meaningful issues that are bothering him, he will eventually suffer. But, used in moderation, the capacity to employ creative distraction is a gift and a sign of emotional intelligence.

When employing distraction (which some people do naturally, others need to do less of, and still others need to learn how to do better), the basic advice is to engage in pleasant, absorbing, and comparatively unexciting activities that do not stimulate more anger, depression, or anxiety.

EXERCISE: Creative Distractions

The list below identifies some tried-and-true distractions that might be useful for your depressed partner. Read through these and check off any that seem worthwhile (or even remotely likely to be received well) to recommend to him. You are not his therapist, but many of these are based on common sense, backed up by research, and (if you catch him in the right mood) may allow you to help him out.

Whenever I recommend various strategies that may be of help to your depressed partner, you have two basic options for how to utilize them: either tell him you read about the techniques in a book and that you'd like him to go over them with you because it might help him; or find some subtle way to encourage him to think or act on these things himself. For instance, "I know you're feeling down, so let's rent some really light comedy together and just try to break the mood." Or "It would be great if you would go out and play soccer with Katie. She'd love it and it would probably do you some good, too."

DISTRACTION TECHNIQUES

- **Absorbing mental activities:** TV, movies, listening to music, reading, video games

  Pros and cons: He feels better because he can't remember exactly why he felt sad or upset, but he needs to be careful about retreating excessively to passive activities like TV or video games.

- **Mood-lifting distractions:** Funny movies, inspiring books, watching sports (as long as his team is winning!)

  Pros and cons: The best distractions actually lift his spirits, but he can't always count on these to be available.

- **Exercise:** Walking, running, working out, team sports

  Pros and cons: One of the best sources of distraction because it is so physical and because it stimulates endorphins, but he needs to be careful of ruminating while working out or of engaging in anger-stimulating activities (punching bag, aggressive basketball game).

■ **Relaxation techniques:** meditation, self-hypnosis, visualization, yoga

Pros and cons: Excellent for cooling down physiologically from anger or anxiety, but not as helpful for depression because there is too much room for unstructured negative mantras.

■ **Personal pleasures:** Massage, Jacuzzi, favorite food, listening to music, sex, buying something

Pros and cons: Anything that activates pleasure can come in very handy—except if it leads to negative consequences (drinking, drugs, overeating, spending money). Also, he needs to be careful about sex as an antidepressant—you may not want to sign up for that.

■ **Accomplishments:** Cleaning the garage, balancing the checkbook, writing a thank-you note, taking care of some phone calls, finally getting the clock right on the VCR

Pros and cons: This activates a feeling of self-efficacy (or personal competence) and distracts him from the unhappiness or powerlessness that he was experiencing.

■ **Helping others:** Playing with his kids, volunteering his time, tutoring, coaching his kid's soccer team

Pros and cons: Helping others reinforces his feeling of being needed and valuable, and also absorbs him in a task separate from ruminating.

Thought Stopping

The classic intervention aimed at negative-thought distraction is known as *thought-stopping*—simply ordering the brain to stop the negative thoughts and get on a different track. Let's look at an example.

Your partner starts worrying about how ineffective he is in dealing with his kids. This self-critique, looping around in his brain hour after hour, has not helped him change his behavior or understand himself better. It is just paralyzing and often brings out even less-effective behavior. Thought-stopping derails this negative cycle by stopping these thoughts. One thought-stopping technique is to snap a rubber band on the wrist and loudly say "Stop!" Try it. The thought chain will be broken. Or try carrying a card with the word "Stop" in bright red letters and looking at it when the ruminating starts. This works very well for some, not as well for others.

What you can do. Make sure he knows about this technique. Sometimes the simplest interventions have an impact. Or, if he is willing, develop a playful secret signal so you can remind him when you notice him heading down the rumination track.

Compartmentalization

Your partner may also find it helpful to employ the technique of *compartmentalization,* or making an appointment with himself to focus on worries only at and for a specific time. He starts to worry. From painful past experience, he knows where the worrying will lead. So he makes a deal with his brain. This appeases the worries. They get the message that they will be attended to, so they don't have to constantly demand attention.

What you can do. Compartmentalization is especially valuable for the depressed man who is also a worrier. And you can help him use it by providing him with a time and place to exercise these worries. Suggest that you can be available to listen to what's worrying him. "I promise to pay attention to what you're worried about, but this isn't a convenient time. Let's schedule in fifteen minutes tonight at seven to talk. I promise to give you my complete and undivided attention for these fifteen minutes." Offer yourself as an audience for the scheduled fifteen-minute worry period. During that period, your job is only to listen to his doubts, obsessions, and regrets. Only respond with questions to help draw him out. Offer no suggestions, no problem solving, no reassuring. Save those for another time. When you help him establish a specific box or compartment like this, you are helping him keep his worries in perspective. The message is "Yes, your worries are to be taken seriously—but they don't have to consume you."

Focusing on Positive Thoughts

A third approach for generating distractions involves specific *focusing on positive thoughts*. The strategy here is to prepare a specific sequence of positive thoughts that can replace the negative ones. He owns those positives, and nobody can take them away from him.

What you can do. Your partner can do this for himself. Some people focus on the positive naturally, others need to discipline themselves to do it. You can also help him. If your depressed partner starts ruminating about something, you should empathize, then remind him of the flip side. For example, if he is ruminating about all the things that are wrong with the kids, you can say something like, "Yeah, I know we can't get Brian to read a book and he's hard to manage at school. It worries me, too. But he's still a great kid in so many ways: a great heart, a quick mind, the best soccer goalie in the district. We have to keep reminding ourselves about these things when he worries us."

NEW HABITS: FAKE IT UNTIL YOU MAKE IT

A central factor in maintaining depression is the man's pattern of depressive guy's habits. Sleeping late. Staying up late. Avoiding social situations. Withdrawing emotionally. Keeping things to himself. Drinking. Compulsively flirting or philandering. Having a messy room, house, car, or workspace. Criticizing you and others. Complaining. And, although many people find this concept foreign, it turns out that one of the most effective components of treatment for depression is the conscious choice to engage in nondepressed guy habits instead. Even if he doesn't feel like it or if it feels unauthentic because it does not spring from an organic process within, jumping into more positive behaviors can help turn a depression around.

Since depression is composed of an interactive cycle of thoughts, feelings, biochemical processes, and behaviors, it turns out that interrupting or changing any of these usually has an impact on the rest. Obviously, if he can change the feelings associated with depression, the other depressive symptoms usually abate. And we see that if he can change his self-talk, the domino effect is likewise powerful. Changing biochemistry through medication, exercise, or herbal remedies will have an impact on the rest.

Changing Depressive Behaviors

The same is true with depression-related behavior patterns. If he starts acting like a nondepressed guy, he is more likely to start feeling like a nondepressed guy. This is partly due to self-image and self-efficacy: "I'm exercising more now like I used to. Depressed guys don't usually do this, so I must be less depressed!" And it is partly because the behaviors which nondepressed guys engage in help to fend off depression. They keep men active, involved, connected, and successful. Or at least offer them just enough of these experiences to feel good enough about themselves and their lives.

What you can do. This strategy for treating depression is simple. Tell him what you have been reading about this, and make this suggestion: "This book on depression that I've been reading says you should just try acting like a nondepressed guy. Just pretend. Let's try remembering times when your behaviors didn't look or feel like depression and revive them—even if you don't feel like it." As with many of these recommendations, you may determine that your partner would feel offended and act defensive if he knew you got these ideas out of a book. You can always approach him just by presenting this like it's a casual idea based on your personal wisdom: "Sometimes it helps just to act like you're feeling up for doing something even if it's not really true. We just have to help get you out of this rut, and maybe your feelings will follow."

Specific and Concrete Instructions

Many men respond best to very specific and concrete instructions about how to pull out of depression rather than more general guidelines and insights. Many women don't make their expectations clear enough; they expect their partner to get it in the ways that they or other women usually understand things.

Divorces initiated by women of depressed men often come at times that are very unexpected for the men, because they have never clearly heard their wives directly asking for the things she needs. Many depressed men are at their best when they are asked for specific, concrete things. Some of the emotional intelligence deficits that many men suffer from require you to spell your needs out for them. Your partner may feel more generous, protective, and effective when he knows precisely how and what to offer you. Even empathy, to a large extent, is a learnable skill. He can act like the nondepressed guy that you fell in love with if you show him what to do. I don't mean to suggest that this is easy and automatic, but "faking it until you make it" has more potential impact than most people think.

For men who have been engaging in behaviors that both reflect and perpetuate the depressive cycle, the assignment is simple to explain (although, obviously, a little more complicated to consistently execute). Guide him into making an effort to try something different, considering it an experiment to see how he feels, what he fears, and how else he can use his time more constructively for himself and others.

What you can do. In a supportive and noncritical way, ask for very specific behaviors from your depressed partner that would really make a difference for you. Always frame these requests positively (what you want instead of critically telling him what he shouldn't do). And if he is reasonably successful at pulling them off, make sure to notice and let him know how much it means to you.

Here are some examples:

- "I would appreciate it if you would not log on to the Internet until you have been home at least one hour. Let's just try it and see."

- "It's important to me that you check your temper at the door when you walk into the house."

- "When the kids want your attention for something, I would really like for you to try to stop everything and offer it to them."

- "I'd really like you to let me know every day something you appreciate about me—even if you're in a bad mood or mad at me for something else."

- "When I tell you something that upsets me, please try saying 'Wow, that must have really worried you' without getting defensive, trying to correct me or problem-solve, or watching a football game at the same time."

- "It would mean a lot to me if you would tell me at least once each day about some emotion you experienced that day—not just anger, but worry, uncertainty, excitement, or pride."

ACTIVATING SOCIAL SUPPORT

One of the most important interventions for anyone who is depressed—and especially for men, who are so much more likely to be self-isolating—is generating and maintaining a healthy social support network.

Utilizing Social Intervention

The first way that this social support can be so valuable is simply to make sure that the depressed man confronts his denial and seeks help for what is going wrong. It will often be the case that you, as his loving partner, can't pull this off by yourself.

It is important to realize that most men seek help only when pressured to do so by significant people in their life, and the single most important thing anyone can do for a man who may have depression is to help him get to a doctor or therapist for a diagnostic evaluation and treatment. You and the other people he cares about can try to talk to him about depression, helping him understand that depression is a common illness among men and is nothing to be ashamed about. Hearing this from another man, a man whom he respects and who has earned his stripes with your partner as a solid guy, is probably the most potent intervention of all.

Empathy, Normalization, and Connection

The second most important thing that his friends and family can offer is basic, old-fashioned emotional support. This involves understanding, patience, affection, and encouragement. They need to engage him in conversation and listen carefully. They need to stay away from disparaging the feelings he may express, instead pointing out realities and offering hope.

Unfortunately, depressed individuals often behave in ways that help assure that their social worlds are less than positive. Not only are they apt to be socially isolated, but research indicates that they often undermine the opportunities for positive social experiences (Wenzlaff 1993). For example, they tend to prefer others who are unhappy like themselves, and they may gravitate toward others who are disapproving of them (in an unconscious attempt to confirm their negative narratives and beliefs). And, most frustratingly to the mega-goals here, they tend to behave in ways that make others unhappy. This makes it harder to attract the social support that is so desperately needed.

What you can do. Remember that what comes easily for you in terms of engaging with other people in your life may not come easily for him, either because of his basic personality, his depression, or both. Encourage him to take small steps to reach out to others in his life and to feel good about these steps (for example, feeling good about a brief phone call he initiates). If you are helping to engineer his increased involvement with other couples, don't throw a huge party. Instead, start with less demanding interactions where social pressure doesn't feel overwhelming, like watching a video or a football game with some friends who are easy to be with socially. You can also help find friends or family members who have been through some version of what he's experiencing and respectfully play "matchmaker." You also can be of help to him by locating a support group for depression through his therapist, his doctor, local mental-health agencies, or your religious organization.

Sometimes you are faced with a very difficult decision about how much to inform others or to involve them in what your partner is going through and what he needs. He may feel extremely protective about his privacy and extremely sensitive about the possibility of looking bad to others. This is completely understandable. However, it is often self-destructive. Although each situation is different, in general I recommend erring on the side of involving others rather than excluding them. And the more serious the depression, the more strongly I recommend this. Of course, you run the risk that your partner will be deeply offended and feel betrayed that you have exposed him, but it is just as likely that he will be relieved. If not immediately, then possibly later.

SUMMARY

One of the most important ways you can be of value to your depressed partner is to understand the range of different strategies and interventions out there (both professionally, like therapy, or more informally, like everyday activities or social support). You can be a gentle ally to him in helping change some of his depressiogenic narratives. You can offer him ideas about ways to distract himself from the most damaging ruminations and negative cognitive patterns. You can also introduce him to the "fake it until you make it" concept in ways that might actually make sense to him. You can help him develop his social support network. The more you know about what has been found to work, the more you can either help him do it or at least be supportive when his therapist or someone else suggests it.

CHAPTER 7

Helping Him with Treatment: Medication

Chapter 6 helped you understand the range of interventions for depressed men including everything except interventions that target the biological and the biochemical.

As with information in the previous chapter, this book is designed to guide all of you who are in a relationship with a depressed man. It is in your best interest to be as knowledgeable as possible about what is out there in terms of antidepressant strategies—in this chapter, the physical, biological, and biochemical. Your capacity to be the most valuable resource for your depressed partner is enhanced when you know about the available interventions: how they work, when they work, when they don't, and what negative outcomes and side effects to be on the lookout for.

THE CHEMICAL NATURE OF DEPRESSION

Depression affects both mind and body, and its origins can certainly stem from either (or both). As you may know, the most powerful biological intervention for depression utilizes antidepressant medication. While it is beyond the scope of this book to review all the different medications in any significant depth, it's important for you to at least have some basic information about the different types of medications, including their advantages and disadvantages.

The chemicals present in the brain that control its functions (thoughts, emotions, motivations, normal and abnormal behaviors) are called *neurotransmitters*. There are a wide variety of these chemicals in the brain, and more are being discovered every year. These various substances transmit information between the nerve cells.

Two of the earliest discovered and most important neurotransmitters are *serotonin* and *norepinephrine*. One important early theory of the biological cause of depression suggested that there was too little serotonin and/or too little norepinephrine in the brains of depressed people. The primary mechanism by which antidepressant drugs work is by relieving the effects of too little serotonin and/or norepinephrine. That is why many antidepressant drugs are called reuptake inhibitors— they prevent the brain from disposing of these necessary chemicals. More recent theories suggest more complex mechanisms for how these drugs relieve depression (and why they take weeks to do so), but inhibiting the reuptake of neurotransmitters undoubtedly plays a role.

How well do antidepressants work in practice? They are used mainly for moderate or severe depressive symptoms. They can be used in combination with psychotherapy, and this combination is often the most effective. One-half to two-thirds of patients who are correctly diagnosed with major depressive disorder will respond to the first drug chosen, and 75 to 80 percent of patients will eventually respond if several different medications are given full trials. Overall, no type of antidepressant drug is more effective than any other, but the different types can have different side effects, and different drugs sometimes are more or less effective for different individuals (University of Michigan Depression Center). The major causes of lack of treatment response include inadequate medication dose or length of treatment and patient nonadherence to treatment recommendations.

CHOOSING A DOCTOR

If your partner is already seeing a therapist or counselor for his depression, it would be natural to assume that this professional could advise him and prescribe medication if necessary. But this assumption is incorrect. Most of the professionals treating depression are not physicians, and therefore they cannot prescribe (nor even give specific advice about) any psychopharmacological interventions.

However, your partner's therapist is a good place to start for getting a referral for a medication evaluation. Every nonmedical therapist works with many patients who are taking medication. And therefore they work with physicians who are prescribing these medications all the time. The therapist should be able to recommend a skilled physician who has solid experience with treating depression through medication.

Psychiatrists work with depression (and the range of other psychological and psychiatric disorders) exclusively, and thus they are most likely to have the greatest range of skills and expertise in these situations. However, many other physicians, including your family doctor or internist, are also very skilled at treating depression. You and your partner should discuss these different issues:

- Do we know (or have we been referred to) a doctor who is really expert in this field?

- Would my partner be more comfortable going to his internist, who already knows him?

- Can we afford the cost of a full evaluation for medication from a psychiatrist?

- What does our health plan cover?

- And, most importantly: Do we feel comfortable with and trusting of this doctor, no matter what his or her specialty?

BECOMING AN INTELLIGENT ADVOCATE

Once your partner has decided to get an evaluation for medication, has chosen a doctor, and has gone in for an appointment, there is some important information to gather about the prescribed medication and the prognosis.

Fist of all, some general guidelines: When people talk to their health-care professionals about the possibility of taking antidepressants, it is important for them to be as fully informed as possible about the medication. Under normal circumstances, since your husband or boyfriend is the one seeking help for himself, you would hand him these guidelines and say to him, "Oh, honey, by the way, when you meet with your psychiatrist, don't forget to go over these items, okay?" And it would be a done deal.

But, with men who are depressed, you cannot always rely on this communication process to take place the way it should. There are two important reasons for this. The first is that your partner is a man, and many men are notoriously reluctant to get a lot of important information from doctors. It's almost as bad as asking for directions. And when dealing with depression, asking a lot of detailed questions about his condition and his treatment regimen only serves to highlight the fact that there is a serious problem. The second is that he is depressed, and people who are depressed are not always thinking as clearly and aren't always as likely to generate the energy that is required to aggressively go after important information in any area of their lives.

EXERCISE: Medication Questions

Every man is different, and every relationship is different. If you believe that your partner can take charge of the information-gathering process successfully, then just pass this list on to him. But if you have doubts, then the following questions outline the areas you need to explore with his doctor.

If you go to the appointment with your partner, or if you get information from the doctor on the phone or via e-mail, make sure you ask these questions:

1.   What do you expect the medication to do?

2.   What is the recommended dosage, and what time of the day should he take it?

3.   How long do you think it will be before we notice any effects?

4.   Are there any interactions with other prescription and non-prescription drugs that we should be concerned about?

5. What about alcohol or other drugs? How will they interact with his medication?

6. How should he check in and let you know about the progress? By phone or e-mail? When is the next face-to-face appointment?

7. How will we know if the medication isn't working?

8. Are there any serious side effects that we should be looking out for? Anything that we should be sure to call you about right away?

9. What about more subtle side effects? Dry mouth? Dizziness? Nausea? Sleep disturbances? Sedation? Irritability?

10. How is this likely to affect his sexual functioning and sexual desire?

BASIC ANTIDEPRESSANT INFORMATION

You will certainly not learn everything there is to know about antidepressant medication from this book. However, it will be helpful to have at least some basic information about the types of antidepressants, the dosages and treatment regimens, and the side effects to look out for. In the Resources section, you can find books and Web sites that give you much more detailed information about each of these areas.

Types of Antidepressants

From the 1960s through the 1980s, *tricyclic antidepressants* (named for their chemical structure) were the first line of treatment for major depression. Though the tricyclics are as effective in treating depression as the newer antidepressants, their side effects are usually more unpleasant. Thus, today tricyclics such as imipramine, amitriptyline, nortriptyline, and desipramine are used as a second- or third-line treatment. Other antidepressants introduced during this period were *monoamine oxidase inhibitors (MAOIs)*. MAOIs are effective for some people with major depression who do not respond to other antidepressants. They are also effective for the treatment of panic disorder and bipolar depression. Because substances in certain foods, beverages, and medications can cause dangerous interactions when combined with MAOIs, people on these agents must adhere to dietary restrictions.

The past decade has seen the introduction of the new wave of antidepressants that so many of you have heard so much about or have been taking yourselves. They work as well as the older ones but have fewer side effects. Some of these medications primarily affect one neurotransmitter, serotonin, and are called *selective serotonin reuptake inhibitors (SSRIs)*. These include fluoxetine (Prozac), sertraline (Zoloft), fluvoxamine (Luvox), paroxetine (Paxil), and citalopram (Celexa).

The late 1990s ushered in new medications that, like the tricyclics, affect both norepinephrine and serotonin but have fewer side effects. These new medications, known as *atypical antidepressants*, include venlafaxine (Effexor) and nefazodone (Serzone). Other, newer medications chemically unrelated to the other antidepressants are the sedating mirtazepine (Remeron) and the more activating bupropion (Wellbutrin).

Dosage and Course of Antidepressants

Dosage of antidepressants varies, depending on the type of drug and the person's body chemistry, age, and body weight. Traditionally, antidepressant dosages are started low and raised gradually over time until the desired effect is reached without the appearance of troublesome side effects. Newer antidepressants may be started at or near therapeutic doses. They typically take one to three weeks to have any benefit, and one to three months for full benefit (University of Michigan Depression Center 2004).

The impact of antidepressants, when they are truly the right match between drug and person, can be dramatic and quick. One male-type depression client of mine, who had to be begged, lectured, and threatened before he finally agreed to try antidepressant medication, came in to a couples session a week later and said: "I realize that I am not as in control of my moods as I thought." This was a huge admission on his part, and it launched a series of changes within him and within his marriage that were nothing but good. Another young man whom I treated because his life was unraveling with temper outbursts and suicide attempts told me only two days after starting Prozac, "I can't believe the person I was even just a few days ago!"

Only a few cases are this dramatic, and the reason why all patients are cautioned to wait a few weeks before expecting positive effects is to ensure that they will continue with the regimen even if they don't notice immediate results. This is smart advice, so please don't expect your partner to change immediately. It is just a powerful lesson about the power of brain chemistry when it does happen this quickly.

Side Effects of Antidepressants

Antidepressants may cause mild, and often temporary, side effects (sometimes referred to as adverse effects) in some people. Typically, these are not serious. However, any reactions or side effects that are unusual, highly annoying, or that interfere with functioning should be reported to the doctor immediately. The most common side effects of tricyclic antidepressants and ways to deal with them are as follows (National Institute of Mental Health 2002):

- *Dry mouth*: It is helpful to drink sips of water or chew sugarless gum.

- *Constipation*: Bran cereals, prunes, fruit, and vegetables should be in the diet.

- *Bladder problems*: Emptying the bladder completely may be difficult, and the urine stream may not be as strong as usual. Older men with enlarged prostate conditions may be at particular risk for this problem. The doctor should be notified if there is any pain.

- *Sexual problems:* Sexual functioning may be impaired. If this is worrisome, it should be discussed with the doctor (more on sexual issues in chapter 8).

- *Blurred vision:* This is usually temporary and will not necessitate new glasses. Glaucoma patients should report any change in vision to the doctor.

- *Dizziness:* Rising from the bed or chair slowly is helpful.

- *Drowsiness as a daytime problem:* This usually passes soon. A person who feels drowsy or sedated should not drive or operate heavy equipment. The more sedating antidepressants are generally taken at bedtime to help sleep and to minimize daytime drowsiness.

- *Increased heart rate:* Pulse rate is often elevated. Older patients should have an electrocardiogram (EKG) before beginning tricyclic treatment.

The newer antidepressants, including SSRIs, have some of the same side effects and some different types, as follows:

- *Sexual problems:* Sexual functioning may be impaired. If this is worrisome, it should be discussed with the doctor (more on sexual issues in chapter 8).

- *Headache:* This will usually go away after a short time.

- *Nausea:* May occur after a dose, but it will disappear quickly.

- *Nervousness and insomnia:* These may occur during the first few weeks. Dosage reductions or time will usually resolve them.

- *Agitation (feeling jittery):* If this happens for the first time after the drug is taken and is more than temporary, the doctor should be notified.

Any of these side effects may be amplified when an SSRI is combined with other medications that affect serotonin. In the most extreme cases, such a combination of medications (for instance, an SSRI and an MAOI) may result in a potentially serious or even fatal "serotonin syndrome," characterized by fever, confusion, muscle rigidity, and cardiac, liver, or kidney problems.

The small number of people for whom MAOIs are the best treatment need to avoid taking decongestants and consuming certain foods that contain high levels of tyramine, such as many cheeses, wines, and pickles. The interaction of tyramine with MAOIs can bring on a sharp increase in blood pressure that can lead to a stroke. The doctor should furnish a complete list of prohibited foods that the individual should carry at all times. Other forms of antidepressants require no food restrictions. MAOIs also should not be combined with other antidepressants, especially SSRIs, due to the risk of serotonin syndrome.

MIND-BODY TREATMENT WITHOUT DRUGS

Not all biological strategies for depression involve traditional medication. Some of the most powerful interventions do target the physical self as a way to eventually target the emotional, cognitive, and behavioral self, but they involve more everyday changes in lifestyle and alternative medicine. Again, it is important for you to be as knowledgeable as possible about these strategies so that you can be an informed adviser and a valuable supporter to your depressed partner.

Physical Exercise

The most potent is physical exercise. Exercise has a great track record in treating depression for four reasons: the physically active man's body is in better condition so he feels good; he feels like he has accomplished something positive and thus defines himself as a self-efficacious person; the intensity of exercise temporarily distracts him from the torrent of depressive rumination—and he gets an endorphin rush!

As described by brain researcher David Servan-Schreiber (2004, 66), the stimulation of endorphins by physical exercise extends far beyond the immediate effects of feeling kind of good about yourself:

> By what mysterious process does exercise have an impact on the emotional brain? Endorphins. The secretion of endorphins brought on by physical exercise stimulates the natural mechanism of pleasure and makes the mechanism more sensitive in general. People who exercise regularly get more pleasure out of the other little things in life: their friendships, their cats, their meals, their hobbies, or even the smiles of passersby on the streets.

What you can do. Simple: do whatever you can to help your partner start—or resume—exercise. Buy him a gym membership and volunteer to do it with him. Encourage his friends to get him out playing tennis or basketball. Remind him of how much better he always feels after he has worked out or been physically active.

Substances

What someone puts into his system, of course, can have a profound impact on depressive symptoms. Men who use cocaine for a while and then discontinue run a higher risk of depression than men who do not. Practically all substances, if abused, increase the risk of depression either during the period of usage or in the period afterwards. The popular party drug ecstasy, for example, stimulates serotonin in the brain (which is why it makes people feel so good) but depletes the capacity of the brain to self-generate the same vital neurotransmitter (which is why users can feel so bad for a while afterwards). And the most widely abused substance of all, alcohol, is chemically a depressant—no matter how happy it makes people at the time that they are getting a buzz on.

What you can do. You can't control what drugs or alcohol your partner uses. Men and women have been finding this out for centuries. But you can limit your own usage, if you recognize that this can have a subtle influence on him. You can insist that his doctor and/or therapist sternly point out to him the dangers of his substance patterns. And you can always simply try the straightforward approach of telling him that you are worried about him and that you would like him to stop or cut back. Or the most straightforward of all: "Stop drinking or I will leave you."

Nutrition

Similarly, we are what we eat. One of the interventions that should always be included in the treatment of depression is an improvement in food-intake patterns. If your partner eats poorly, his mood is likely to suffer, and if he eats well, he at least won't be swimming upstream when using all the other interventions and strategies that he may be employing.

Furthermore, researchers are now beginning to discover a link between mood disorders and the presence of low concentrations of omega-3 fatty acids in the body. Apparently, omega-3s help regulate mental-health problems because they enhance the ability of brain-cell receptors to comprehend mood-related signals from other neurons in the brain. In other words, the omega-3s are believed to help keep the brain's entire traffic pattern of thoughts, reactions, and reflexes running smoothly and efficiently. Clinical trials are underway to further investigate whether supplementing the diet with omega-3s will reduce mild to moderate depression and bipolar disorder.

What you can do. Eat well. Cook intelligently. Stock the refrigerator with good nutrition in mind. Foods a depressed man should eliminate or eat in moderation include sugary foods and caffeine. He should get in the habit of eating at least three times a day, including breakfast, replace sweets with fruit and whole-grain carbohydrates, eat lean sources of protein several times a day, and drink plenty of water. Focus on a well-balanced diet, including plenty of leafy greens for folic acid, and bananas, avocado, chicken, greens, and whole grains for B_6.

Good sources of omega-3 fatty acids may be found from Atlantic salmon and other fatty, preferably cold-water fish, including herring, sardines, Atlantic halibut, bluefish, tuna, and Atlantic mackerel. As a reasonable substitute (or even an occasional alternative) for fresh fish, commercial fish-oil capsules are available containing omega-3s such as DHA and EPA. Canola oil, flaxseed, flaxseed oil, walnuts, and leafy green vegetables such as purslane are all good sources of alpha-linolenic acid (ALA), the plant-based omega-3. A quarter-cup (1 ounce) of walnuts supplies about 2 grams of plant-based omega-3 fatty acids, slightly more than is found in 3 ounces of salmon (Whole-HealthMD 2005).

Alternative Medicine

One other area to make sure you are all aware of includes alternative medical interventions. Because of the widespread interest and positive anecdotal reports about Saint-John's-wort, the National Institutes of Health (NIH) conducted a three-year study comparing patients with major depression of moderate severity receiving either a uniform dose of Saint-John's-wort, an SSRI, or a placebo (a pill that looks exactly like the SSRI and the Saint-John's-wort, but has no active ingredients; National Institute of Mental Health 2000). The scale measuring overall functioning and levels of depression was better for the antidepressant than for either the Saint-John's-wort or placebo. While this study did not support the use of Saint-John's-wort in the treatment of major depression, ongoing NIH-supported research is examining a possible role for Saint-John's-wort in the treatment of milder forms of depression. Some other herbal supplements frequently used that have not been evaluated in large-scale clinical trials are ephedra, gingko biloba, echinacea, and ginseng.

What you can do. Stay on top of this research, because it is changing all the time. Try talking to your partner's doctor about these, although many physicians are very cynical about alternative medicine. Talk to other people you know who have tried some of these and see if someone can recommend a homeopath, acupuncturist, or someone else who knows this field. For more information and Web sites about alternative medicine, please check the Resources section.

HELP HIM MAKE CHANGES

Everything in this chapter involves potentially positive biochemical interventions or lifestyle changes that can be of tremendous benefit to your depressed partner. But, ultimately, it is his choice and his alone whether to purse these. Your role involves the following four behaviors—which can make it more likely, but not guaranteed, that he will follow through:

- *Encourage and educate:* The more you know about medications, side effects, the effects of exercise, the effects of nutrition, etc., the more you can pass on to him. You can show him an article you read or something you pulled off the Internet that gives tips about these choices. Your partner may not be acquainted with the information because he may not be motivated to seek it out himself, but, in many cases, he may value what you present to him.

- *Join him:* If you want to help your partner work out more, join a club with him. If you want him to eat more intelligently, make the same changes in your own diet. If you want him to cut back on excessive alcohol or Starbucks, do the same. The purpose here is to make it as easy as possible for him to be successful at his own treatment program. You have to know your own limits, and you may not be able or willing to make the same changes that you are hoping he makes. But do it wherever you can.

- *Restructure the environment:* Behavioral psychologists know that changing behavior not only requires reinforcing positive behaviors and challenging cognitions, but also usually requires some form of restructuring the environment. The simple goal of all of these approaches is to increase the likelihood of success. If his and your goal is for him to eat more wild salmon (with its omega-3 fatty acids), then do whatever you can to make sure it is ready and available in the refrigerator. If alcohol intake is a problem, try to avoid settings where excessive alcohol consumption is de rigueur. If he is sloppy about taking his medications daily, set up a pill divider system and lay it out for him so it requires no other thinking or effort on his part. Buy him a great new racquetball racket to make it more likely that he will want to play.

- *Words and attitudes:* What you communicate to him, directly or accidentally, about his program is likely to have much more impact than you realize. If you make it sound like a burden on the family to have fewer sweets around the house, he is likely to use that as an excuse to blow his plan. If you make some cynical comment about people who need medication to get through the day, he will feel shamed and resist the medication regimen that he needs. If you roll your eyes about quack doctors who offer gingko biloba, he will think it's stupid, too.

SUMMARY

The biological, physical, and biochemical interventions for depression are sometimes absolutely primary and always at least worth considering. To help your partner stay informed and make intelligent decisions about them, you both need to know basic information about the biochemistry of depression and about the vast range of antidepressant medications. Finding the right doctor and asking the right questions are both crucial. It is also essential to be aware of the lifestyle factors that may be having a profound effect on his depression, such as exercise, substance abuse, and nutrition. With problems as complex as depression, it is also definitely worth considering alternative medicine interventions.

CHAPTER 8

Intimacy Issues: Sexual and Emotional

There are two different kinds of intimacy: physical intimacy, or the sexual relationship, and emotional intimacy, or the ways in which two people are open, honest, real, and connected with each other. Depression affects intimacy. And problems (or successes) with intimacy affect depression.

In this chapter, you will learn about how your sexual relationship with your partner may be affected by his depression, as well as how his treatment (especially antidepressant medication) may have an impact on sexuality and sexual performance. You will also learn about the barriers to emotional intimacy that may be fueling his depression and how to help reduce those barriers to make it more likely for genuine emotional authenticity and intimacy to emerge. This is not easy and usually not reducible to a formula or quick-fix intervention. But the potential payoffs are enormous for the three targets of this book: him, you, and the relationship.

SEX AND MALE DEPRESSION

Men who are suffering from depression are likely to lose interest in sex—or gain interest in sex. They are likely to feel more easily threatened or jealous. And they are more likely to see sex as the simple solution that will be the miracle drug alleviating all their distress.

When He Loses Interest

It's very common for depressed men to lose interest in sex (Phillips and Slaughter 2000). Although there are hundreds of reasons why a man might show a reduced interest in sex (temporary stress, problems with physical health, reactions to medication, deterioration of the relationship, simple aging, hormonal disturbances, etc.), depression is one common possibility to consider. Depression depresses the sex drive.

This decreasing interest in sex is usually a nasty blow to your partner's self-image. A man who loses interest in his sexual relationship with you, or has interest in the concept but can't achieve or maintain an erection, is not going to feel good about himself. Observing and labeling himself as a failure in the bedroom is one of the last things you would ever wish for a man, and definitely one of the last things you'd want for a man who is already depressed.

When his sex drive diminishes, there are two reactions that typically happen. The first is that he will blame himself. He will feel ashamed and that he is less than a man. He'll worry that he is profoundly disappointing and failing you, and that you will not love him or be attracted to him anymore. He will withdraw from you in shame.

Or, whether he withdraws in shame or not, he may blame you. He blames because he cannot comprehend or bear the pain of feeling like such a failure. So he feels propelled into desperately seeking another explanation for this devastating problem: "It must be her! She's just not attractive anymore since she gained weight. She doesn't give me enough attention. She has hurt me, and I don't even want to look at her," and so on. He may feel justified in seeking out an affair, and the novelty and feeling of conquest may recharge his sexual batteries for a while—further proving, in his mind, that his equipment works fine and that you were the problem all along.

What you can do: If your partner is feeling bad about himself without blaming you, the most loving and generous response you can offer him is simply your fundamental support, patience, and love. If you understand what is happening for him, you can find ways to avoid taking it personally. If you make it personal, you'll just make both of you feel worse. Your self-talk is crucial; here are some things you can say to yourself:

- "This is not the same sexually driven man I have always known, but that's what depression does."

- "This is not the same sexually driven man I have always known—that's what antidepressants can do."

- "I know what it's like to have a sex drive that waxes and wanes. This is not about me or my attractiveness."

- "He's feeling very bad about this already. I have to do everything I can to make sure he doesn't feel even worse or more guilty."

If your partner has turned to blaming you, your task is more complicated. Either (or both) of you can always find something wrong with you if you're looking for it—because no one is perfect. Who among us has not gained a few pounds? Who among us is not quite as attracted to our partner as we were in the courting and honeymoon stages?

His depressive projections of blame onto you are toxic for him, for you, and for the relationship. It is your job to not let yourself fall victim to this by accepting blame or responsibility. You may acknowledge certain criticisms that are accurate without buying the whole package:

- "Well, honey, maybe you're right. I could pay more attention to you. Maybe that would help some. I just don't want you to put the whole problem on me."

- "I probably could put more effort into setting the mood for sex, and I'll try to do that. But I'll feel more sexy, too, when I feel less blame from you."

You also need to respectfully and assertively stand firm and challenge his narrative about his loss of sexual interest:

- "I am not the perfect wife, but I'm not chopped liver, either. No offense, but you're not the perfect husband. We're in this

together, and it's unfair for you to blame me because you
aren't interested in sex anymore."

- "I want to work on this with you, but I can't feel safe if you are
  intent on blaming me."

It would not be in the least uncommon if, in the past, you became
frustrated because your partner did not understand fluctuations in
your sex drive. Now that the tables are turned, you might find yourself feeling deeply hurt, anxious, and sometimes angry. Some people
even think that a man who isn't chomping at the bit for sex is some-
how less masculine. If this shoe fits for you, it's important that you
pay close attention to the narrative you're telling yourself about the
situation and your resulting responses. Unless you are convinced that
your partner is engaging in a hostile retaliation by withholding sex or
that he is getting his sexual needs met elsewhere, it is essential that
you give him the benefit of the doubt and remember how frustrating it
can feel to be the misunderstood party. Be patient and don't take it
personally—which is exactly what I tell men when the shoe is on the
other foot. Here are some narratives that can help you:

- "I know what it's like to have less sexual interest than my
  partner. I also know how you can misread that and make more
  of it than it really is. I don't want to do that to him."

- "I have to admit, I feel like a real man simply wouldn't be
  losing interest in sex. I know that's kind of dumb, and I don't
  want that to get in the way of how I respond to him."

- "I can't help it. It hurts my feelings to be rejected. But I have
  to stay on top of this. There are too many important things at
  stake to let my hurt feelings mess things up further."

When He Gets Too Interested

Another symptom of male-type depression is an acceleration of
sex drive. Sometimes this is related to a swing into a manic phase of a
bipolar disorder. More typically, it represents a desperate (and usually
unconscious) attempt to fend off depression and the subsequent
feelings of unmanliness.

In this pattern, you may see that your partner is using sex to self-soothe. Many covertly depressed men cling to the knowledge that there is at least one sure-fire (if temporary) relief from the storm clouds of depression. This relief (unlike medication, self-help, therapy, etc.) feels profoundly masculine and has a quick and powerful impact on a physical level, a biochemical level, a self-esteem level, and (usually) on an emotional level. Just as alcohol "works" for many people to dull the ache, so does sex.

And if sex sometimes feels good, why not sex all the time? Every day. Twice a day. With different partners. With different partners at the same time. Watching porn at the same time. With some risk involved, like in a closet at a party or in the same hotel room with sleeping kids.

Many men who meet the criteria for sexual addiction patterns are fundamentally depressed at the core. They have turned to the rush of sex and the hunt for more sex to escape an inner emptiness.

I saw a couple in my office for marriage counseling who were on the brink of divorce because of the husband's ongoing affair. As he related his narrative of the deterioration of the marriage, he blamed first and foremost his wife's lack of affection and diminished interest in sex over their twenty years together. This common complaint from men seemed like a legitimate issue to explore—until it became clear that he wanted sex daily, often twice daily, and that his evidence of his wife's "diminished interest in sex" meant that she only wanted to have sex twice a week! There is nothing wrong with wanting frequent sex; individual sex drives cover a vast range. But for a man to cheat on his wife of twenty years and break up his family because she "only" wanted to have sex twice a week has all the markings of a sexual addiction—and a desperate attempt to escape a deep, covert depression.

What you can do: Don't let yourself feel guilty for not providing the profound soothing that your partner is seeking through sex. Too many expectations about what sex provides can ruin something that should be wonderful and fulfilling. Your role is to negotiate between your natural sex drive and his, sometimes compromising, sometimes insisting on following your own needs. That's it. And when he tells you that he wouldn't be so depressed if you just would put out more, don't buy it. Here are more narratives to help you:

- "I know he keeps telling me that his only problem is that I won't have as much sex as he needs, but I know that's not true."

■ "Our sex drives are different. I want to compromise and offer more of what he wants, and he needs to do the same for me. I know he'll like it if we plan out a certain night as our time together, and I'd be okay with that too."

■ "It is not my job to make him feel better through sex."

■ "I don't respond well when I feel like he needs me or needs sex so much. It's got to be something that is only one part of our relationship, not the biggest thing."

And, certainly, if his craving for sex leads him to engage in behavior that is unacceptable in your marriage contract (such as having affairs or engaging in reckless sexual behaviors with you), then you should draw a line in the sand and leave him if he can't or won't change (see chapter 11).

When He Gets Jealous

It stands to reason that when a man is feeling bad about himself, it becomes more and more difficult for him to believe that you or anyone else finds him desirable and attractive. If you combine this with the pattern of projecting blame for personal unhappiness so prevalent in male-type depression, you have a cocktail for jealousy and possessiveness.

My client Malcolm had been struggling with male-type depression off and on for several years. He had become increasingly unhappy with his wife, Laura, and increasingly had been blaming her for his moodiness.

Their sex life had been deteriorating for several years because of his depression, his alienating behaviors, and another little factor known as having two kids under the age of seven. During the course of their marital therapy, some aspects of the relationship began to improve. And one Saturday night, Laura surprisingly (even to herself) seduced Malcolm and became more passionate than she had in many months.

You might think this would have been a good thing, that it probably was a relief, a reassurance, and even an antidepressant to Malcolm. Instead, within an hour after engaging in great sex with his wife, he withdrew into one of his moods. Then he lashed out at her, saying, "The only reason you're enjoying sex with me is because you're imagining being with someone else! You must be cheating on me!"

When we peeled off the layers of this very painful encounter, we found destructive self-talk from Malcolm. He said to himself, "She couldn't really be that attracted to me. I'm just not lovable. I think she's about to abandon me now, when I'm at my lowest. No one loves me except my son."

Another client of mine, wife to a depressed man, reported a chillingly painful interchange between her and her husband. He was complaining to her that she never gave enough attention to him, sexual or otherwise. Then, as she was heading out to a kid's birthday party with her five-year-old son, her husband called out, "There you go again with your boyfriend" (referring to her spending time with their five-year-old son). And he said this within earshot of the boy.

What you can do: The guidelines for how to respond to these behavior patterns of male-type depression, which spring from insecurity and fears of abandonment, echo the advice that you have been hearing throughout this book. Try to be understanding about what he is going through, try to be as reassuring as possible, and don't take any crap.

Men who are going through this experience of insecurity and self-doubt are easily bruised fruit, and it's in the best interest of him, you, and the relationship to gently remind him of the simplest messages frequently. For instance, "I love you. You are very attractive to me. I know you worry about this sometimes, but I am not interested in anybody else."

And if his insecurity and jealousy issues are expressed in directly hostile or destructive behaviors, like in the examples above, he needs a firm message from you that you will not accept this abuse. Some men actually appreciate limit-setting when they are spinning out of control. Others refuse limits and simply increase their belligerence, which may escalate to a level where you have no decent choice but to leave the relationship (see chapter 11).

Sex as a Simple Solution

A lot of women complain that their husbands get way too focused on sex, saying things like, "Don't you see that if you just had sex with me more often I wouldn't be so depressed?" or "Okay, now that I'm communicating better and being nicer, it's your turn to reciprocate and offer more sex."

What you can do: You are not a vending machine. Your partner can't just put in a couple of quarters and expect a soda or a bag of chips. However, it is usually true that if he's able to come through with more of the relationship behaviors that are positive, affectionate, supportive, helpful, and understanding, then you are more likely to feel sexual. A standard line that women's magazines typically suggest is to tell your partner things like, "Foreplay is washing the dishes." Not making sex a specific reward, but being more amenable to sex just because you feel closer to him and less resentful.

For many men, making love (and especially the positive mirror of being in a relationship with a woman who wants to make love with him) is a cornerstone of their sense of well-being. It won't cure a clinical depression, but it sure doesn't hurt. And making love usually helps men feel connected, which is a good thing. So it benefits both of you and the relationship if you try to move sex to as high a priority on your list as you can without faking it or being disrespectful to yourself. You may find it helpful to pull out your own bag of tricks to help stimulate your sexual interest: lighting candles, talking about sexual fantasies, making sure the kids are out of the house, going out dancing together, giving each other massages—even cleaning out the garage together, if that works for you. Or consider any of the other thousand techniques that you may run across in women's magazines or books or just may have discovered about yourself along the way.

ANTIDEPRESSANT MEDICATION AND SEX

It seems a little unfair, but just when your partner finally recognizes that he is suffering emotionally, acknowledges it to you, seeks professional help, agrees to try out antidepressant medication, and actually notices some positive benefits, that's the time when he starts to notice a drop in his libido and sexual performance. The most popular and effective antidepressants, the SSRIs, lead to some degree of sexual side effects in as many as 60 percent of men (Zajecka, Mitchell, and Fawcett 1997). Considering how important sex is to male self-image and sense of well-being—and how important a healthy sex life is in most relationships—this sexual side effect can spell trouble.

Common Side Effects

The two most common sexual side effects that are caused by SSRIs include delayed ejaculation and absent or delayed orgasm. A reduction in sexual desire is also very common, although it is difficult to determine whether this is a direct side effect or an obvious psychological reaction to the fact that sex is not as easy or as satisfying. It is a natural psychological reaction to avoid, or at least be less attracted to, experiences which are no longer as rewarding as they once were. Doctors don't always explain to men the possible loss of libido. So it's easy for a man (who is not very likely to inquire about these matters or discuss them with his friends) to start wondering whether or not he still loves his partner. "After all," he may think, "if I'm no longer aroused by her I must not love her anymore!"

Treatment Options

It is usually advisable for your partner to wait a while before switching medications. Sometimes the sexual side effects turn out to be avoidable. Some people build up a tolerance to the medication, and the sexual side effects disappear. Your partner's doctor may recommend altering the timing or dosage of the medication or switching to another medication that may have fewer sexual side effects.

For example, Wellbutrin SR (an antidepressant, but not an SSRI) is an alternate medication for depression. Wellbutrin SR can sometimes alleviate the sexual side effects caused by SSRIs, when taken in combination with the SSRI or when used instead of the SSRI. Effexor, another atypical antidepressant, generally causes fewer sexual side effects than most SSRIs. Serzone generally does not cause sexual side effects, but may cause sleepiness or upset stomach. By the time you read this, there will probably be more options.

Drug Holiday

A "drug holiday" is another strategy for maximizing the impact of the antidepressants while managing the sexual side effects. It means that the patient takes a temporary break from their medication. For example, the patient stops taking the SSRI on Thursday morning and resumes taking it on Sunday afternoon, hopefully finding himself without the sexual side effects for the weekend. This does not work with certain medications, and the plan can be totally derailed if he forgets to resume the medication on time, or if he likes to be more sexually active during the week than on the weekends. No matter what, he should only try this after careful consultation with his doctor.

Talking About the Problem

It can be very difficult for your partner to initiate a conversation with a doctor about sex—especially when he feels like his equipment is not working right. Men have a wide range of reactions to antidepressants, and even the best of doctors cannot help navigate the terrain without detailed information.

This is another situation where you, as his ally and personal observer, can help identify and articulate the changes that have been taking place for him. You can help provide an additional perspective.

One way to help you both analyze the information and to name the concerns about sexuality is to compare what things were like before the depression started, during the depression, and after antidepressant treatment kicked into gear.

EXERCISE: Tracking Sexual Interest

The following questions are adapted from a form developed for the American Association of Marriage and Family Therapists in an information packet for the public entitled *Intimacy and Depression: The Silent Epidemic* (2004). Go ahead and answer them in your journal.

To try to make sense of the possible sexual side effects from your partner's antidepressant medication, try to track (with his help or simply from your own observations) the information you cull from these questions. Much of these data, of course, can be affected by many other factors, such as life circumstances, emotional issues in the relationship, medical conditions, etc. But at least you'll gain some guideline information to help determine whether there is a correlation between the medication and sexual problems.

You don't need to use exact numbers (like number of minutes and seconds until ejaculation!). Just make some notes in response to each heading about this particular aspect of his sexual response. After he has been taking antidepressants for a few weeks, you should keep track of these factors for at least a month or two. This will help you put the possible sexual side effects in perspective. If you realize from gathering this information that his sexual response is really different, you should definitely encourage him to talk to his doctor. He may decide that the side effects are tolerable when compared with the positive effects of the medication overall, but it may be possible to make some adjustments so that neither of you have to deal with a blow to your sex life.

SEXUAL INTEREST (frequency, general interest, masturbating)

Before Depression _____

When Depression Most Prominent _____

A Few Weeks After Taking Antidepressants _____

BECOMING AROUSED (achieving erection, maintaining erection)

Before Depression _____

When Depression Most Prominent _____

A Few Weeks After Taking Antidepressants _____

STAYING AROUSED (erection sufficient for penetration)

Before Depression _____

When Depression Most Prominent _____

A Few Weeks After Taking Antidepressants _____

REACHING ORGASM (ability/time for reaching orgasm)

Before Depression _____

When Depression Most Prominent _____

A Few Weeks After Taking Antidepressants _____

What you can do: As with so many of these subjects, knowledge is power. The narrative you use at the times when your partner loses sexual interest is crucial. If it really makes sense to you that this is related to his antidepressant medication, then you have the option of trying to problem-solve using some of the strategies described above or at least not to take it so personally, especially when doing so leads you to feel bad, critical, angry, and blaming of yourself.

For your partner and for you, the decision about dealing with the sexual side effects from antidepressants may ultimately come down to a cost-benefit ratio. Can he benefit significantly from antidepressant medication? And, if he can, but it interferes with his sexual interest and responsiveness, is it worth it? Sometimes it may be, at least for a while, compared to the alternative. Can the two of you find a middle ground?

BEYOND SEX: AUTHENTICITY AND EMOTIONAL INTIMACY

All of the techniques and strategies offered in this book are designed to help you, your partner, and your relationship. Sometimes these interventions won't fit the bill. Or they may be helpful but not exactly on target. But the most powerful path, the one that may have the most profound impact, lies on the path of looking within. For him, and also for you.

Sometimes the most powerful antidepressant path involves a journey toward personal authenticity and emotional intimacy. And, by embarking on this path, your partner may find that depression is often absolutely incompatible with authenticity and intimacy. Why? Because, for many men, the core of depression is an alienated sense of self. Many men have disowned their inner self in a desperate attempt to ward off unbearable or unacceptable emotions. Sometimes, because of a life crisis or personal maturity or finding the right audience (therapist, spouse, etc.), a man is able to drop his mask and face issues in himself that he's never been able to face before. The energy that used to go into fighting this authenticity was feeding the depression syndrome. If he has the courage and good fortune to be truly authentic about his feelings, he may cry or feel hurt or vulnerable. But accepting and feeling his real emotions is not depression. It's just real.

Authenticity breeds the capacity for intimacy, and intimacy, in turn, generates authenticity. As the great psychologist Carl Jung once said: "One is always in the dark about one's own personality. One needs others to get to know oneself" (1977, 165).

You can't do this for him, of course—but you can help.

Authenticity

Authenticity, for the man in your life who is depressed, means that he is not bullshitting himself. It is defined by researchers Colarusso and Nemiroff as "accepting what is real in both the external and inner world, regardless of the narcissistic injury involved" (1981, 86).

The "narcissistic injury" referred to above means that your partner is able to see himself clearly and take responsibility for his own feelings and behaviors *even if it makes him feel bad.* Even if it does not conform to his self-image. Even if it makes him look bad to you or others.

My client Daniel, intermittently depressed and moody for years, precipitated a marital crisis when, in a fit of unhappiness and frustration, he picked up an ash try and threw it at his wife. She needed fourteen stitches. Months later, as they were trying to reconstruct this broken marriage, she accused him of rolling his eyes when she asked him to do something around the house for her.

Daniel was outraged and responded with "I was feeling so warm toward her, and I was complimenting her and everything. How could I have rolled my eyes and done anything that was mean or condescending?"

This is the narcissistic injury. "How could I? How dare she?" And it interfered with his capacity for authenticity. The man who is authentic with himself in this marital encounter would tell himself, "Get a clue, man! You're certainly capable of contradictory feelings toward the same person—even (especially!) the person you most love, the person you depend on the most, and the person with whom you are most vulnerable."

Or the simple version, "Maybe she's right."

Mickey, on the other hand, figured out how to do the "authenticity thing." His chronic depression had led him to alcoholism and infidelity, in a desperate search for the rush of adrenaline and endorphins that he craved. When it all came crashing down and he came close to losing his marriage, he grabbed himself by the collar, threw himself against the wall, and told himself to get it together and act like a man. He joined AA and went into therapy. He began the process, made famous in AA groups, of taking a "personal inventory" and worked at recognizing his fundamental helplessness and personal defects.

Mickey told me that he felt like he'd been born again. He wasn't talking religion, per se, but rather the religious experience of authenticity. He paraphrased Bob Dylan with "I'm invisible now—I've got no secrets to conceal!" As his wife slowly began trusting him again and warmed to his reborn self, Mickey had the epiphany that being real is sexy!

Many years ago, when my fiancée and I called off our wedding three weeks before the date, I plunged into depression. I started to see a psychotherapist to make sense of what had happened and to help keep me glued together. Somewhere in the midst of one of my long, whiny litanies about how cruel my ex had been to me, my therapist stopped me short and said, "You're the one who was really aggressive to her. You were sneaky about it, but you did plenty of it yourself." This was not what I was paying the big bucks to hear. I feebly protested, then slunk into feeling ashamed and more depressed, this time for being a fool.

And then, in a matter of hours, I felt a lot better. I knew he was right. Suddenly, with the cloud cover removed, I was able to see myself as a much more flawed person than I had allowed myself to see before. I felt freer, and I felt the depressive and stuck moods just peel away in layers. I still had a lot of work to do, but I wasn't feeling depressed. I took a step forward in the life task of the "gradual acceptance of the self as imperfect" (Colarusso and Nemiroff 1981, 86).

Emotional Intimacy

With authenticity comes the capacity for true intimacy. Intimacy involves your partner's capacity to be authentic with you and the other specially chosen people in his life. But especially with you. It also requires that he relax his standards for you. He develops the ability to see you, like himself, not as an idealized partner but as a real person: *She ain't perfect—and neither am I.* True intimacy is another invaluable antidepressant.

Another client of mine, Keith, had been mired in a depression for several years. He withdrew more and more from his wife and eventually had an affair that blew up the marriage. As we dissected what had gone wrong, he put it together like this:

> *I just got more and more vaguely dissatisfied with the relationship because I couldn't be real. Holly, so wonderful in so many ways, always had this image of how I was supposed to be. She needed me to be successful and churchgoing. We were supposed to be young, attractive, successful, wonderful people on the right path in life. There was very little margin of error. I was dazzled by the ride that our life together offered me, but I ignored the problems. I just sunk into depression and eventually pushed her away without paying any attention to what I was doing. I think it might have been really different if I had been able to tell her more of these things when they were happening. But I felt like I didn't know how to be myself.*

Keith is describing the central experience in Terrence Real's description of covert male depression: the shutting down of the emotional world, and the shutting down of access to genuine interpersonal connection as a result (1997). Keith knows now that this dynamic fed the particularly male-type depression that unraveled his relationship.

Factual Honesty vs. Emotional Honesty

When I ask people if they think they are being truly honest in their relationship, most people claim that they are. Unless they are deliberately withholding important information from their partners, most people of reasonable integrity can genuinely claim that they are honest. But there are two kinds of honesty in a relationship. Only the first involves facts.

My client Julian spent years feeling run over by his wife. She spent money more extravagantly than he wanted. She insisted on only buying certain foods for the home, even though he wanted some of the "forbidden" ones. He privately grumbled and sometimes bickered with his wife, but he never really brought up his unhappiness about these patterns in direct and assertive ways.

Then one day he found himself in the middle of an affair. And when his wife demanded to know why he was cheating, all he could come up with was that the affair "just helped me feel better." He was not lying about the facts. He was simply not being fully truthful about the inner experiences that generated his behaviors.

This other kind of honesty is more difficult to quantify. I call it *emotional honesty*. This kind of honesty reflects the capacity, the willingness, and the courage required for your partner (or for you, too) to report his genuine inner world to you. It means that he's willing to be honest about how he's feeling. For example, if he's acting cold and you ask him if he's mad, he would confirm the reality by acknowledging, "Yeah, I am kind of upset with you for what you said at that party," instead of saying, "No. What are you talking about? I'm just feeling a little tired—is there something wrong with that?" The lack of emotional truthfulness is depressiogenic, while working to be more emotionally honest can serve as an antidepressant.

Please don't get the wrong idea: I do not advocate that people in relationships act as though they are in a 24/7 encounter group where they report their feelings all the time. It's boring to live like that, and no successful couple that I know of actually operates in that fashion. But the practice of sharing feelings of competition, hurt, self-doubt, anxiety, jealousy, and even excitement are the lifeblood of relationships. If your partner doesn't know his own feelings, if he knows them but lacks the words to express them, or if he knows how to express them but is afraid to, then he is short-changing you, himself, and the relationship.

A man knowing his own feelings is a sign of authenticity and expressing them is a sign of intimacy. Something's wrong when these are lacking. But here's the good news: it's not that hard for men to get better at this.

What you can do: You may need to be very clear about what you mean when you tell your husband or boyfriend that you don't believe him. Be careful about making an accusation that will feel like an insult to him. You may know exactly what you mean, but he may not. He may think that you are accusing him of lying to you, which outrages any man who considers himself to be an honorable person. When women say, "I don't believe you" to a partner, they often mean that they suspect he's not being straight about what he is feeling or what his motivations are for a certain behavior—why he is withdrawing, moody, getting critical, etc.

If you are careful to downplay language that may activate his broken mirror, then you can reasonably expect him to learn how to identify and express his emotions at least a little more.

LEARNING AUTHENTICITY AND INTIMACY

As a loving, pro-relationship gesture, there is a lot you can do to help your male partner develop increased authenticity and intimacy. You can help teach him what is called distress tolerance and the value of experiencing necessary losses.

Distress Tolerance

Marsha Linehan defines *distress tolerance* as "learning how to bear pain skillfully" (1993, 96). Borrowing from the wisdom of Zen Buddhism, she advocates the development of mindfulness skills, including the non-judgmental observation of one's present emotional state, however distressing it may be. For instance, when finding yourself in a distressing but unavoidable situation, you might think something like, "I can't do anything for now to change how I feel or to change the situation, so it's better to accept this for now rather than do something to make things worse." This capacity to tolerate painful feelings is an essential ingredient in emotional intelligence, and a deficiency in this skill is depressiogenic.

My client James described it this way:

I have noticed a real change in myself. Ever since this affair and everything I have learned about myself, I can listen to my wife more openly. Sometimes something will set her off, and she'll get some worry or question or suspicion in her head and she gets a little crazy. And I used to be so defensive when she got that way. Why? Because I felt terrible about myself, and seeing her so unhappy would just remind me of this.

But now I can handle the distress better. When she gets into that state, I remind myself that I have really messed with her head and with our marriage. And I have confidence that she, and we, will get through it. Feeling bad for a while is not so terrible, and it allows me to really talk to her and not shut her out. It's making such a difference!

When James says that "feeling bad for a while is not so terrible," he is describing his newfound capacity for distress tolerance. Feeling depressed is not that big a deal. He doesn't have to run. He doesn't have to pretend it's not happening. He doesn't have to defend against it. He doesn't have to counterattack. He is strong enough to tolerate feeling bad and confident enough to know that it will pass—in fact, it's a hell of a lot more likely to pass if he can bear the pain skillfully.

What you can do: You can offer your husband or boyfriend a real gift if you can reassure him that feeling bad for a while is not that big a deal. You can remind him that, even though you are mad at him or feeling distant, this too shall pass. He will be able to handle depressive periods better if he remembers that they are temporary and fleeting, and that they do not always require an immediate escape plan.

Necessary Losses

Judith Viorst's 1996 book, *Necessary Losses*, advances the concept that all change and growth require losses of some sort. And even though these losses are never attractive or appealing, they are as inevitable as rain. They serve as opportunities for growth. People can either fight them (usually futilely) or learn from them.

Many of the stories that I've described in these chapters have involved a man who ran headlong, kicking and screaming, into his own version of depression and the destructive effects of his moods, thinking, and behaviors.

What if, instead, he could look at a distressing transition and see an available lesson? His kids not turning out the way he envisioned?

Very painful and challenging, but potentially a lesson in over-attachment. He finds that he sinks into moods and blames others? Very toxic to his most intimate relationships, but offers the opportunity to understand himself better and take more responsibility for his life. He continues to feel self-doubting about his work or how others view him? Very depressing, but offers him the chance to discover that the most important judge of himself is himself.

What you can do: Your partner may not be very receptive to hearing this perspective from you, because the very nature of depressive moods and thinking patterns lead to resistance to generating a more positive perspective. But when you can slip it in, with your impeccable timing and finesse, it can be very helpful to suggest to him that he can use these difficult times to become a deeper, more knowledgeable, and more compassionate person. (This is especially credible if you are doing the same yourself.) For instance, you might say something like the following:

- "Honey, I know you're really worried about all the pressure you've been getting from work, and you are really doubting yourself. Please don't take this the wrong way—but maybe this isn't such a bad thing. You're learning a lot about yourself, and you're learning more about how to handle it when things don't go well."

- "I know that it's really hard for you to hear about Luke having all these problems at school, and you blame yourself a lot. But maybe there's some lesson here for both of us about not getting so attached to how our kids are supposed to be."

BE CAREFUL WHAT YOU WISH FOR

Are you sure you really want this more authentic guy? The question always reminds me of the movie *When a Man Loves a Woman*, in which Meg Ryan plays the role of a closet alcoholic who eventually becomes sober—and a lot less fun. Her husband (played by Andy Garcia) becomes more and more frustrated because she is no longer quite the fun party girl she used to be.

When my kids were young and not yet verbal, people would watch them and say, "Don't you just wonder what they're thinking?" I remember that, in fact, I wasn't particularly interested and that it was actually kind of nice not having to know.

The authentic guy you have always craved may be more vulnerable. He may have more fears or doubts. He may not conform to your vision of who he is supposed to be, whether that means going to church or not going to church, making a great income, or having a more relaxed lifestyle. He may be less sexually charged than he used to be, and maybe you miss his sexual dynamism. Or maybe his sexuality wakes up, and you suddenly feel overwhelmed. When he changes the depressive or moody behaviors that have always been so difficult to live with, it is nothing but good. But this transition may be accompanied by other changes that may force you to face your own expectations—of how a man in your life is supposed to act, of the kind of life you have always wanted to have, or even your expectation of yourself.

SUMMARY

Intimacy issues in relationships (both physical and emotional) can either be a cause of depression or a fallout from it. When depressed, some men withdraw from sex, others turn to it excessively. Antidepressant medication can also have a major effect on sexual interest and functioning. Furthermore, a man's capacity to be emotionally authentic can help him cope with and fend off depression, and his capacity for authenticity can lead to a more genuine capacity for emotional intimacy with you. You can play an important role in helping him navigate the changes in his sexuality and in helping to elicit his authenticity and true intimacy, all of which can serve as profound antidepressants.

CHAPTER 9

Guilt and Expectations

When living with a depressed person, especially someone with the classic male-type depression characteristics of hostility and blame, it is almost impossible not to feel guilty. You may feel guilty for not being able to protect him from feeling bad, for not being the perfect partner, and/or for getting angry or impatient with him when he's depressed.

Sometimes, experiencing guilt is a healthy function. It represents our God-given gift to examine our own behavior, experience some remorse, and reform ourselves into better people. But excessive guilt is your enemy for three reasons:

1. It makes you feel bad—a lot worse than you deserve.

2. It enables your partner to continue in his depression-driven patterns of blame.

3. It makes you angry. Most people I know who feel guilt in their relationships also feel angry about being made to feel guilty. This anger often leads to destructive and hostile behavior—which makes them feel even more guilty.

IT'S NOT YOUR FAULT

Depression loves company, and depression often stimulates the projection of blame. A man who is depressed and who cannot successfully identify, tolerate, or take responsibility for what he is going through often has a remarkable capacity to make his partner feel as if it's all her fault. It's as if there is no other rational explanation for his level of unhappiness or moodiness than an external one: "*You* must be making me feel this way."

Emotional Reasoning

At a certain noninsightful level, this may technically be true. But this represents an error in thinking known as *emotional reasoning,* which is best defined as someone making conclusions about themselves or others simply because they have a particular feeling. It may be that your criticism of your partner for his emotional withdrawal, your reduced interest in soothing him sexually, or your frustration with his negativity and criticism may actually be leading him to feel bad. But if your partner blames you for these feelings, he is probably engaging in this classic dysfunctional narrative. Just because your actions or words have led him to feel bad does not mean you *intended* for him to feel that way, nor does it mean that he *shouldn't* be feeling a little bad.

You are likely to feel guilty if, in his emotional reasoning, he blames you for hurting him or making him feel bad. But you need to do your own "gut check" to see if you are guilty as charged. If you're not, it's best to refuse to take on this guilty baggage. In one couple I counseled, the wife confronted her husband about his excessive moodiness. He didn't deny that he had a problem. He didn't deny that it was destructive to her and to the family. He just responded in classic blaming, defensive fashion, "I wouldn't feel so bad about myself if you just treated me better." Because he felt bad, she must have been treating him badly.

In this situation, *you* might be tempted to resort to emotional reasoning: "Since I feel guilty, there must be something wrong with me."

But it doesn't have to stay this way. A female client of mine described the conversation she had with her male-type depressed husband after years of feeling bad for not taking better care of him emotionally. In full blaming mode, he yelled at her, "You have made me miserable for sixteen years of our marriage and you cannot make me happy!"

Finally, after years of feeling guilty, an accelerating marital crisis, and several months of therapy, she calmly replied: "You're right, Carl, I can't." Period. End of sentence. Sadness, but not guilt.

"You Are a Bitch"

He may accuse you of being too critical of him. He may acknowledge that your criticisms have some validity, but say that you always bring them up at the wrong time, or in the wrong way. When he is engaged in full defensive mode, you are very likely to end up feeling like the bitch.

Again, it's important to do a gut check. Maybe you need to review some of the lessons from chapters 3 and 4 about communicating most respectfully and effectively. But, for many men, there is no such thing as the right time or the right way. It all feels like an assault, and you will always be blamed. You are not likely to be perfect at communication, but perfection is not necessary for a successful relationship. "Good enough and trying to get better" is plenty, and if he consistently tries to make you feel as if your imperfect communication is the central problem, you should not buy in.

Making You Feel Stupid

Another pattern of blaming you involves his communication pattern aimed at making you feel stupid. And, if you are like 99 percent of the population (male or female), you are vulnerable to the possibility that you are not quite bright enough, or informed enough, or able to use higher-level reasoning enough, or articulate enough. When you get this message consistently from someone you fundamentally trust and love, it can start to get to you.

Your partner may even be right. It is certainly possible that he has a few IQ points on you, or that he knows more about certain subjects. So what?

My client Raul (in a role reversal from many other male-female relationships) gave his wife books on relationship skills, ostensibly to help her. But she always experienced this action as a veiled form of criticism that he would never acknowledge. When she would complain that this felt like a put-down and that she didn't appreciate his self-improvement suggestions, he acted like she was just being too sensitive: "What are you talking about? I'm just trying to help." If there is anything worse than someone trying to improve you, it's someone trying to improve you and denying that they are doing so.

And then there is Susan, a successful and well-educated business-woman married to a very successful and intellectually gifted attorney. Her husband, mired in male-type depression, consistently complained that she was not well-informed enough and not able to figure out problems that involved analytic reasoning, like programming technology. In tears, she told me, "I have never ever questioned my intellect until I got into this relationship with my husband. Now I worry all the time about being stupid and failing him in the process."

EXERCISE: When He Blames You

In the exercise below, ask yourself about ways your partner tries to make you feel guilty or inadequate. Try to be honest with yourself. Are his criticisms completely justified? Are they totally from outer space? Are they somewhat true, but nowhere near as serious as he is making them out to be? You may want to ask someone who knows both of you to help you get a reality check.

Then, based on your assessment, activate self-talk to put the complaint in perspective. Here are some examples:

- *On Target:* "He's right. This is something I really need to work on."

- *From outer space:* "I refuse to take responsibility for his depression and unhappiness."

- *True, but exaggerated:* "Okay, I see some of that, but he is trying to make this out to be all my fault, and I will not accept that."

DOES YOUR DEPRESSED PARTNER . . .	On Target	From Outer Space	True, but Exaggerated
Tell you that you expect too much from him?			
Tell you that he wouldn't be so depressed if you would just have more sex with him?			
Accuse you of paying more attention to the kids than to him?			
Criticize you for bringing up problems at the wrong time?			
Criticize you for bringing up problems with the wrong language?			
Consistently complain about how much you've changed for the worse over the course of the relationship?			
Accuse you of making "suggestions" but denying that they are criticisms?			

EMOTIONAL BLACKMAIL

Sometimes the guilt you experience in your relationship with your depressed partner does not emerge in response to direct ways that he makes you feel bad about yourself. Instead, you may experience guilt when he feels really bad about himself.

Sometimes these guilty feelings emerge naturally, with no intent on his part. But other times your partner may find ways to subtly and passive-aggressively make you feel sorry for him in a way that controls your mood and behavior.

The Threat of Suicide

The most obvious and destructive form of this is the suicidal threat: "I will kill myself if you leave me." He may be saying this in all sincerity, simply stating the facts. Or he may be saying this in a desperate, manipulative, and calculated way—knowing that you would never want the blood on your hands if he actually did something so horrible to himself and to you.

No matter what his motivations, it is extremely important that you keep close track of your own self-talk at this point. If he kills himself, as awful as this would be on a thousand different levels and to a thousand different people, it would be his decision, not yours, and his fault, not yours.

When you have your own narrative straight in your mind, you are then equipped to deal with this challenge in the way you have been hearing about again and again throughout this book. You'll be able to be clear about what you need in a way that is least likely to be punishing or destructive to him. For instance, "I pray that you would never do something so horrible to yourself. I would miss you terribly, and so would many others. But if you choose to do this, it will not be because of me, and I will not live my life in fear that you might take that step."

The Threat of Feeling Horrible

Another form of manipulation (again, sometimes consciously intended and sometimes not) takes place when your husband or boyfriend describes how bad he feels, then retreats into painful guilt and excessive self-recrimination. The emphasis here is on the word "excessive."

For example, my client Aaron, moody and depressed, came into the couples therapy session saying that he really wanted to hear some of the things about his behavior patterns that were bothering his wife. So far, so good. She was reluctant, because Aaron had a history of defensiveness and counterattack when she brought up issues like this. But, with my guidance as their therapist, she gingerly told him some of the hurt and resentment she had been keeping in.

Aaron did not become defensive. He did not counterattack. Instead he went the other direction, saying, "Oh my God! Everything you say is true. I have been a horrible husband to you. You don't deserve this. I screw everything up. I can't see how you can stay in this relationship, because I know I'll never be able to change."

Some of you may be thinking that this could be a good thing, and that it would be nice for Aaron's wife to hear this. But she hated it. She found herself starting to console him, telling him that it was not as bad as he was making it out to be.

And, of course, it really wasn't. But the net effect of his self-flagellation was the same as if he had yelled, threatened, or pouted: Aaron's wife shut up and shut down. She ended up feeling like she couldn't tell him this kind of information without precipitating this over-the-top reaction in him. She wanted Aaron to take her concerns seriously, but she didn't want him to become devastated. She felt guilty for making him feel bad. And she was left with the nagging realization that, just when the spotlight was on her to talk about her feelings, Aaron had found a way to get the spotlight back on to him and what he was going through.

I don't think Aaron consciously planned out this maneuver, but that didn't change the effect. His wife's best response? Assertively insist that the communication pattern change, something like, "Aaron, wait. You're taking this too far. When you get so devastated, I feel like I can't tell you these things. Let's try this again, and I just want you to listen to what's bothering me, let me know if you get it, and maybe try to problem-solve. That's all."

EXERCISE: Responses to Emotional Blackmail

When your depressed partner makes statements to you that are consciously or unconsciously designed to make you feel sorry for him and back off from doing what you need to do, you need to have some assertive responses ready. Here are some examples. Fill in the remaining boxes with other examples you have heard and what would be a good and healthy response.

EMOTIONAL BLACKMAIL	GOOD RESPONSE
"I will kill myself if you leave me."	"That would be horrible, but it would be your choice, not mine."
"I know that nobody loves me."	"I don't think that's true, and I want you to know that being upset with you doesn't mean that I don't love you."
"I can never do right for you and the kids—this just proves it."	"I want you to be able to hear what I have to say without making it worse than it is."
"You're right—I do terrible things. I don't know why you stay with me!"	"Some of the things you have done have been very hurtful to me. But I stay with you because I love you. That doesn't mean I'll stop calling you on it when you are treating me badly."

FEELING GUILTY ABOUT WITHDRAWING

Many of you, even those of you who so desperately insist that you want the man in your life to communicate more and to express more of his inner self, may become anxious when he expresses more about his depression. Many of you may complain that he stays emotionally hidden, yet you may end up feeling threatened about the possibility that he is "weakening" when you hear or see more of his doubts and insecurity.

Withdrawing Because He Seems Less Attractive

Almost without exception, depressed men are simply less attractive than men who are less depressed. And they are especially unattractive because many of the depressive emotions and behaviors (or the lack of certain behaviors) run so counter to traditional masculine traits. Depressed people are generally more tentative, indecisive, unmotivated, and emotionally dependent. When women are depressed with these traits, they feel awful and it's not much fun for their partners. But when men sink into these states, they are profoundly violating the guy code. As a woman in this man's life, it is absolutely essential that you recognize your own expectations and reactions. You have to acknowledge your own reactions even if you dislike seeing yourself as a woman who would feel this way.

Withdrawing Because You Can't Rely on Him

It also can be quite disconcerting having to take care of someone who has always taken care of you. If you have always relied on your male partner as a pillar of strength and he starts to crumble before your eyes, you're likely to feel not only worried and compassionate but also resentful and betrayed. He may withdraw socially, he may be more self-centered and less attentive to what you need from him, and he may be less able or motivated to make a good living.

While you may be the most understanding and compassionate person in the entire world, you're still human. And we humans cannot help but be affected by our personal needs. This is not a crime and not a sign of a character flaw in you. It is human for you to feel resentful when some of what you have counted on from your partner changes and evaporates. It only becomes destructive to the relationship if you don't know what you are feeling, if you feel so guilty about it that you pretend you aren't feeling it, or if you suddenly, inexplicably, find yourself attracted to someone else without understanding why. Your job is to be accepting of yourself and to stay conscious. Thoughts and feelings do not necessarily have to dictate actions.

Withdrawing Because He Treats You Badly

Some of you who are especially prone to feeling guilty may feel like you have failed when you withdraw from your partner, no matter what the reason or how justified this withdrawal may be. A pattern I often see in relationships with male-type depression goes like this:

1. As his male-type depression emerges, he becomes more moody, irritable, and blaming.

2. She feels emotionally beat up and withdraws from him emotionally, behaviorally, and sexually.

3. With his depleted emotional resources and blaming tendencies, he resents her for not being there when he needs her.

4. She feels guilty—she has failed in her nurturer role and made her suffering partner feel even worse.

5. She tries harder to please and support him, and (in this emotional climate) it is never enough.

If he is treating you badly, it is only natural to withdraw for emotional self-preservation, not to mention personal pride. This is not a guilt-worthy dynamic.

THE SEDUCTIVE APPEAL OF THE WOUNDED MAN

Although the fight-or-flight model (and the accompanying sympathetic nervous system arousal) has developed as our best model for explaining the behavior of people feeling threatened or stressed, a new model for explaining female reactions to stress and threat is also starting to emerge. This is called the *tend-and-befriend* model (Azar 2000). While this pattern does not supercede the fight-or-flight response, it is significant enough in women to help explain the seductive appeal of the wounded man.

The tend-and-befriend model suggests that women, rather than fighting or fleeing from stress, tend to respond to stress by tending to themselves and their young and by befriending others. Women in stressful situations respond with nurturing behaviors (the "tend" part of the model) and by forming alliances with a social group (the "befriend" part of the model).

When you see your partner hurting, you may find that your instincts tell you to do everything you can to soothe, nurture, and befriend. This is a wonderful instinct—very human and especially, biologically, very female. The problem with it is that it may keep many of you in caretaker/nurturer roles long beyond what's healthy. At some point, tend-and-befriend should be balanced with assertiveness, boundary-setting, and tough love. And, as you will see in chapter 11, this instinct may keep you in emotionally destructive, dysfunctional relationships long after you should have taken better care of yourself.

This pattern may be especially true for you if you have a personal history of being a caretaker in your family growing up. Andrea, who grew up with an alcoholic father who she was always desperately trying to please and keep happy, put it very simply when she described her role in her marriage to her depressed husband: "I have always felt the need to rescue him. And I always thought this was a good thing. I guess it is and it's not."

You're more likely to be seduced by the appeal of a wounded man if you have grown up believing, consciously or unconsciously, that bringing out the best in a man was your life mission. You must know yourself and learn (from trial and error and lots of feedback from others), when your nurturing instincts are generous and loving and when they are codependent and dysfunctional.

SUMMARY

It is very easy to feel guilty when living with a depressed partner. This is especially true for women because the role of nurturer is so deeply embedded in female consciousness and expectations. While guilt comes in handy sometimes, it is destructive when your partner plays mind games to make you feel guilty for his moods and unhappiness. Many men resort to a sophisticated form of emotional blackmail to elicit the guilt of their partners. It is also easy to feel guilty when you find yourself withdrawing from the emotional demands of being in a troubled relationship with a male-type depression partner. This may be especially challenging for you because of your susceptibility, as a woman, to the seductive appeal of a wounded man.

CHAPTER 10

Taking Care of Yourself

Your partner is depressed. He may have symptoms of typical or male-type depression, and you're feeling worried about him, emotionally beat up, and burned out. He may show signs of bipolar depression, and his swings from scary depression to reckless manic episodes may take all of the energy and coping skills you have in your repertoire.

As a loving partner, it is easy to become consumed by trying to stay attuned to him and to deal with his moods and emotional demands. In this situation, it's easy to forget about yourself. But, just like the instructions you hear in the airplane-safety presentation, "Place the oxygen mask over your own mouth before placing the mask on your children," you're not going to be of much use to him, to yourself, or to the relationship if you let yourself deteriorate or detonate.

ASSESSING YOURSELF

The first step in developing an action plan for how to take care of yourself involves a personal assessment. You need to know how you have been affected in your personal behavior, in your thoughts and feelings, and in the way you are relating to others.

EXERCISE:
Assessing the Impact on You

Your life with your depressed partner may be affected negatively in a number of different ways. The charts below, divided into the three main areas, list questions you can ask yourself to make sure you understand yourself and what is happening. Place a check mark in the column for each question indicating not at all, a little, or a lot.

This is not a test with certain cutoff scores. If you answer "a lot" to any of these, it is important simply to be aware of it and possibly to take some action to deal with it. The action part comes next. But first, the self-assessment.

CHANGES IN YOUR PERSONAL BEHAVIOR	Not At All	A Little	A Lot
Has anybody told you that you seem different lately?			
Does it seem like you're not performing as well at work, with your kids, or in any other areas of your life?			
Do you feel like you are "walking on eggshells" around your partner?			
Have you had to make changes in your life to accommodate your partner's moods or behavior changes?			
Cutting back on work?			
Changing your social life or activities?			
Withdrawing from friends?			
Keeping the kids away from your partner at times?			
Sleeping more or sleeping less?			

Lifestyle changes because of financial setbacks?			
Have the basic patterns around the house, such as morning routines or mealtimes, become more disorganized?			

RECOGNIZING YOUR THOUGHTS AND FEELINGS	Not At All	A Little	A Lot
How did you feel when you realized that your partner was depressed?			
Worried?			
Sad?			
Guilty?			
Angry?			
Embarrassed?			
Other _____ ?			
Have your feelings changed? How do you feel about it right now?			
Worried?			
Sad?			
Guilty?			
Angry?			
Embarrassed?			
Other _____ ?			
Does it seem that to you that this is not the man you thought you were getting involved with?			
Do you feel trapped or resentful?			

	Not At All	A Little	A Lot
Do you resent the way he has become more dependent on you?			
Do you worry that your actions will just make the situation worse?			
Are you worrying about what's going to happen in the future?			
Are you feeling more distracted and finding it difficult to concentrate?			
Do you have escape fantasies, like just wanting to walk out the door and never come back?			
Do you worry that your partner can't be trusted to be responsible for your kids?			
Have you lost your feelings of being attracted to your partner?			

RELATING TO OTHERS	Not At All	A Little	A Lot
Are you keeping all of your feelings to yourself?			
Do you find yourself covering for your partner when others are concerned or upset with him?			
Do you feel you have neglected other family members because of the depression?			
When you talk to other people, does it seem like they often tell you that you're just worrying too much?			
Does it bother you when friends or family tell you how to fix the problem (as if you haven't thought of these ideas yourself)?			
Are you flirting more with other men?			

STRATEGIES FOR TAKING CARE OF YOURSELF

If you scored "a lot" on many of the items in the survey above, then it is essential—for you, for him, and for the relationship—that you activate as many self-care strategies as you possibly can.

Many of these strategies you already use, but it may be helpful to review them so you can use them more regularly and more comprehensively. Go ahead and disregard any that don't fit. Many of them seem pretty simple and ordinary, but it is valuable to be reminded of the simple and ordinary if they have value. Certainly, many of them are quite generic and could apply to almost anyone going through any kind of stress or crisis, while others are very specific to being in a relationship with a depressed man.

Perspective Strategies

As you know from the examples in this book, the information you have and the perspective you use can make a huge difference. Here are some guidelines, first of all, for ways to think about the situation.

Educate yourself. Read books. Talk to people. Check out Web sites. The more you know about what is happening to your partner and about how this often affects relationships, the less victimized by the experience you're likely to be. You need a context. You need to know what to expect and what not to expect, and you need to know your options. Information can help you feel more empowered in a situation that is ripe for feelings of powerlessness.

Know yourself. It is essential that you pay very close attention to your own thoughts, feelings, motivations, and expectations. You don't want your own reactions to catch you by surprise or sneak into your relationship patterns any more than they have to.

Anticipate his depressiogenic situations. The worst impact on you (not to mention your partner) from his bad moods, withdrawn behavior, and hopelessness takes place when you have no clue or warning. Pay attention to the patterns: Does his depression get worse in social situations? Does he seem overwhelmed by the kids? Does he withdraw when he can't perform sexually? Is he most blaming of you when you have been distracted and less attentive to him? If you can see some of this coming—although you may not be able to prevent it—you may at least be able to prepare yourself for it psychologically.

Maintain perspective. Moods usually come and go. You decided to hitch your wagon to this man because you saw so many wonderful things in him and felt love and admiration for him. Try to keep these in mind as you weather some of the rough times. And when you set boundaries or insist on certain changes from him, remember that this work will benefit you both.

Practice the art of nonattachment. Ridiculous as this may sound when we are talking about someone you are so deeply attached to, you need to constantly remind yourself that his moods, his life decisions, his relationships, and his decisions about his medical and mental-health care are ultimately his own. You can help, beg, encourage, threaten, and worry, but ultimately he needs to take care of his side of the street.

Social Strategies

Here are some more strategies for how to gain strength, sufferance, and perspective from those around you.

Open up to friends and family. You can't do this alone. The oldest form of coping with stress in the long history of civilization is talking to other people about what you're going through. You need to complain. You need to cry. You need to tell someone about the times when you don't think you can take it anymore. You need to have someone you trust remind you about the times when things were better or help give you some hope for the future. And often these specially chosen allies in your life can generate specific strategies or provide you with information that can help guide you through this difficult terrain.

Choose the right people. Although the healing effects you'll gain from talking to other people are potentially enormous, you'll have to choose carefully. Some people may give you crummy advice, either because they are poor listeners or because they have been through their own troubled relationships and can't see yours clearly and distinctively enough. Other people may be blabbermouths who will not be respectful of your privacy. And others will simply be people to whom it would be too humiliating for your partner to have been exposed. You always have to weigh the advantages to you of having these conversations and the potential harm to him, and then decide based on your own particular weighing of the variables in this equation. Sometimes he'll prefer you to avoid the topic with some people, but it can't be helped, and other times it is vital that you respect his needs.

Be careful not to overwhelm others. You are experiencing distress because of what your partner and your relationship are going through, and you need to talk to the key people in your life about it. Your partner, whom you can usually talk to about things that are tough for you, can't deal with these conversations because it makes him feel guilty, anxious, or resentful. Although your friends and family will be there for you, be careful not to burn them out. Your sister loves you, but she may not be able to talk with you on the phone every day about your emotional state. Try to share the burden among a few people.

Try professional support. You may find it valuable to reach outside your support circle. Many people in your situation see a therapist for emotional support, education about what is happening, and guidelines about how to proceed. It can sometimes be an incredible relief to talk to someone about your situation without worrying about rumors being spread, damaging the person's view of your partner, or judgment about yourself and how you are handling the situation. The same is true for support groups. In almost any city or town of even moderate size, there exists a network of self-help or professional support groups. Some are generic in terms of the problems that are being discussed, while others may be very specific to having a loved one who is experiencing depression. Check the Resources section at the end of this book for ideas about how to find a therapist or a support group in your area.

Relationship Strategies

Here are strategies that focus on specific ways to take care of yourself in this troubled relationship.

Establish clear and firm limits. The single most important step to take in the world of self-care in a relationship with a depressed man is to establish boundaries. For example, "I will not let you talk to me that way." "Even if you are feeling depressed, I still need you to pick up the kids and to do your share of the housework." "I know you feel very private about all of this, but I have to be able to talk to my sister about what we're going through or I'll go out of my mind." As you've read throughout this book, love and compassion is great, but your reluctance to establish limits will destroy you and enable him. Many people who have trouble setting limits sink into depression themselves or erupt, unpredictably, into some sort of "I'm mad as hell and not going to take it anymore" behavior (like an affair).

Help him develop independence. It should be obvious why it is helpful for your partner to develop and maintain as much independence and personal competence as possible, even when he feels like withdrawing and giving up. But it's also important for you. Your despair and resentment are both key players here, and you want to do everything you can to keep these at bay. If you end up cooking, shopping, cleaning, parenting, and making up excuses socially for your depressed partner far beyond what you consider to be fair or tolerable, then danger lurks. You will worry about him and will feel resentful. If you become excessively resentful (the key word here is "excessively"), it will tear you apart and you will not be able to be any kind of decent or generous ally to him. If you set boundaries and hold him accountable, your resentment will stay more manageable.

Deal with your own sexual frustration. Here's a controversial subject, and one where the experience differs widely from partner to partner. Many women who are in relationships with depressed men watch as the sexual connection in the relationship slips further and further into oblivion. As you know by now, this can result from both the man's depression-driven anhedonia and loss of self-esteem and from the wear and tear on the relationship because of increased conflict and emotional distance. Or your sex life may be struggling because of antidepressant medication. For some of you, the loss of the sexual connection may not be that significant. You may miss it, but you have much bigger fish to fry when it comes to what you are worried about in your partner's behavior and in the relationship. If this fits you, then the temporary loss of the sexual relationship is bearable.

Others of you may experience this loss with enormous sadness and frustration, which could propel you into an affair. The basic advice here is to be very careful about seeking sexual satisfaction with another person. You may be opening up a wound in your primary relationship that can never be healed. Instead, this is a time to use all of your personal resources, including masturbation, enjoying the experience of nonsexual touch with your partner and others, and feeling good about your physical self through exercise, yoga, massage, etc. For more guidelines about personal narratives during sexual slumps, see chapter 8. For guidance about when you may reach a point where you can no longer stay in this relationship as it is, see chapter 11.

Behavioral Strategies

Another set of self-care strategies involve specific behavior patterns or lifestyle changes.

Keep a journal. The power of putting your thoughts on paper (or, in modern times, on a laptop) has been recognized for centuries. Nothing changes—except for your experience of the stress and challenges you're going through, and that is no small thing. Keeping a journal in which you pour your heart out can help you get through some of the toughest times and remind you of who you are and what you've got.

Take care of yourself physically. The wear and tear of dealing with a troubled partner and being in a stressful relationship can erode your immune system and trigger an array of physical distress in you. You have to find ways to keep yourself healthy and strong: eating well, exercising, staying away from any abuse of substances, stuffing yourself full of vitamins and healthy supplements. You can't help him if you are depleted yourself.

Use your relaxation response. Another central coping strategy is to find a way to stay emotionally, physically, and spiritually centered. Your mind knows ways to calm the alarm systems in your body, and the various forms of meditation, breathing, and centering techniques can help remind you of this. There are thousands of them. One of the best and most user-friendly is the "mindfulness meditation" popularized by Jon Kabat-Zinn (1990). Kabat-Zinn presents several meditation techniques that focus attention, whether it's on a simple phrase, your breathing, or various parts of your body. This promotes mind/body awareness and calms the nervous system, promoting a feeling of inner stillness and relaxation. It changes your perception of events that cause stress.

Maintain routines. During times of stress and chaos, maintaining the primary structures of your life can be a very valuable coping strategy. Keep regular bedtimes. Eat meals as a family as you always have. Your mind and body will appreciate the sense of stability that results. Above all, try not to let your partner's depression and moodiness significantly alter what you and your family do. Everybody needs to know that the basic routines of life will always continue, regardless of temporary conditions.

Keep up with hobbies and recreation. Not only does depression generate anhedonia, but living with someone who is depressed does the same. It is important that you keep doing the activities that are meaningful and fun for you (except the ones that have destructive side effects, like hanging out in all-night bars). Your conscious and unconscious self need a consistent reminder that your partner's struggles are only a part of your life—they do not govern all of who you are nor what you are capable of experiencing.

Pray. If you are so inclined, pray. Pray a lot. Pray for his recovery and healing. Pray for your own. Pray for patience and fortitude and creative uses of your personal resources. And pray that you will learn and grow as a result of what you and your partner are going through.

SUMMARY

When you're trying to take care of or react to a depressed and often difficult partner, it's easy to lose track of yourself and what you need. First, you need to take a personal inventory to discover the ways in which you are being affected by your relationship with your partner: changes in your personal behavior, changes in your thoughts and feelings, and changes in how you are relating to others. Based on this assessment, it is essential that you activate your wide array of coping resources: self-talk, social, relationship, and behavioral. You deserve to take care of yourself, and, at the least, feeling better will provide you a better chance of being a valuable partner to him as well.

CHAPTER 11

Knowing When to Leave

This final chapter may not apply to all of you. Many of you need guidance in dealing with the challenges of being in a relationship with a depressed partner. But it in no way seems bad enough to break up the relationship, nor has the possibility of leaving him ever been a serious question in your mind.

Some of you, however, have reached this point, and you may be struggling with the toughest decision of all: under what conditions does it make sense to leave your depressed partner? No answer here can ever be complete or perfect. This chapter can, however, help you recognize your own limits and needs—balancing respect for yourself, for him, and for the relationship as you struggle with these tough choices.

MAKING A DECISION

In any problem situation, whether it is a suffering relationship, an uncomfortable job environment, or a car that is giving you problems, you're faced with three basic options. And most of us, almost automatically, go through these three options like a decision tree. We start with the first, and if it doesn't work, we go to the second. If even that doesn't work, then and only then do we go to the third option.

Changing the Situation

The first option, of course, is to try to change the problem situation. In the case of living with a depressed man, this means helping him with his depressed moods, confronting him about ways that he's not treating you well, getting him to engage more socially in ways that will be meaningful and fun for him, and so on.

If this is successful, then life gets a lot easier for him, for you, and for the relationship. You don't need to take any further steps, because the core problem has changed. I truly hope that this first step alone is successful.

Adjusting Your Expectations

If step one doesn't go a long way toward solving your problem, it's time for option two. This means changing yourself. You can gain a sense of control and peace with the situation by adjusting your expectations, learning to appreciate your half-full glass, and finding ways to take care of yourself so that the negative effects of his problems do not wipe you out so much.

Most of us have done this often in our relationships. As humans, we are remarkably flexible, and adapting like this does not necessarily indicate codependency, denial, or low self-esteem. Successful couples do this all the time, and in many situations (not all) it is just plain smart.

Leaving the Situation

Sometimes even this second option is beyond your reach. Option three, then, is to leave the situation. In your case, that means leaving the relationship. I hope that you do not reach this level. This chapter is designed to help you decide whether or not you have.

In trying to make these decisions, and certainly in pursuing the first two options, make absolutely sure to try couples therapy. First of all, you have to feel confident that your therapist is good. If things don't get better over an extended period of time (six months or more), try another therapist just to be sure. If things still fail to improve, then the future of the relationship looks pretty bleak.

COMPETING INNER VOICES

Most of you could make a very good case for why it makes sense to stay in your relationship and work things out (you probably wouldn't bother reading this book if you didn't think so), and many of you could also make a good case for why it would actually be a better and more emotionally honest choice to leave. You are balancing very decent values and inner voices in ways that happen to compete with each other.

On the one hand, you tell yourself that staying is the right thing to do. You might think something like, "Commitment is good. I signed up 'til death do us part.'" "Staying together for the kids is good." "I don't think I'd really be any happier alone."

On the other hand, sometimes you feel like leaving is right. That sounds more like, "I deserve better than this." "I don't want to be a caretaker all my life. This is just too exhausting." "Even though he is a good man, I can't ever forgive some of the ways he has hurt me and burdened me."

You try to listen to the true voice within—except you're not sure which one is the true one. This chapter will help you ask the right questions to put these decisions in perspective. But remember, neither my advice nor anyone else's can ever make the right choice for you.

The dilemma, when you consider the possibility of leaving your depressed partner, is not a choice between living with him versus being perfectly free and happy. It is a choice between living with these challenges versus all the challenges and benefits being single again would bring. Perhaps you'd feel relieved of a tremendous responsibility, but you'd also be facing life with new burdens. These might include being a single mom, divorced, financially worse off, emotionally and sexually alone, feeling like a failure for being part of a marriage that did not succeed, hearing the disapproval of your parents, hurting and/or provoking your partner, dealing with the aftereffects on your kids from this rupture in their lives, etc.

If, given these choices, you think it all through and decide that the pendulum still swings toward leaving, then this is the best decision. Even though you can never be sure, you can be at peace with your choice if you have deeply, sincerely, and carefully considered what your real options are.

INTENSITY, FREQUENCY, DURATION

Most research about disturbing symptoms of any kind, from headaches to marital arguments, assess the symptoms according to three dimensions: intensity, frequency, and duration. A change in the right direction on any of these dimensions is progress. Significant change on all three is worthy of celebration. In order to assess whether the problems you are experiencing in your relationship are serious enough to cause you to leave, it makes sense to think along all three of these dimensions.

Contract Violations: Intensity

Let's start with what we can say with a reasonable amount of certainty, although there are exceptions even here. If the depressed man in your life is physically abusing you, it almost always makes sense to leave. It doesn't matter if you feel sorry for him, or if you know that his depression is really what's behind this unruly behavior, or if his father abused him and his mother ran off with her pimp. The abuse is impossible to live with.

The same could be said for other serious breakdowns in the relationship contract. We all have these contracts, even if they are never written, spoken, or even within our conscious awareness. Most of us have at least implicit contracts that neither we nor our partners will abuse each other physically, verbally, or behaviorally. And most of us agree that we will not betray each other by sharing ourselves intimately with another, by violating the confidentiality of our deepest secrets or vulnerabilities, or by turning against the other in profoundly offensive or hurtful ways. Contract violations leave wounds that are often unable to heal, making it impossible for the relationship to resume and be what either partner needs it to be.

In some ways, the most intense contract violations are a welcome event, if only because they help to clear the clouds of doubt and ambivalence you may have about staying. Sometimes it is actually easier when a partner does something really awful, so you can leave with clarity and in good conscience.

These are the pretty easy criteria. But even these have exceptions. For example, your male-type depressed husband or boyfriend may have cheated on you. For practically everyone, this is a contract violation of high intensity. In other words, it is really bad—not just an annoyance. And for some of you, there is no way to ever recover. But for others, your assessment of his level of remorse and his commitment to change may allow you to stay in the relationship despite this intense violation.

The most important assignment you have regarding high-intensity negativity from your partner is to draw a line in the sand.

EXERCISE:
Where is Your Line in the Sand?

We all put up with lots of imperfections and annoying behaviors in our partners. The capacity to do this is usually a sign of personal strength, maturity, and love. But some behaviors are so profoundly unacceptable that they should never be tolerated, or at least never tolerated more than once. When you draw a line in the sand, you are making a contract with yourself that you will absolutely leave this relationship under certain conditions. When you put it in writing, and you sign it, you are more likely to have the perspective and courage to follow through if the situation actually happens.

I will have no choice but to leave my partner if he ever (cheats on me, hits me, abuses the children, lies to me about his gambling, makes another suicide attempt, visits child-porn sites, etc.)

1. _____

2. _____

3. _____

In addition to these large, obvious transgressions, I won't put up with certain other behaviors. I will have no choice but to leave my partner if he ever (stops talking to me for weeks on end, refuses to find a job, forbids me to talk on the phone with my friends or family, etc.)

1. _____

2. _____

3. _____

_____   _____

Your signature   Date

"Good Enough": Frequency

"Good enough" is a term originally coined in studies of mother-child interactions (Winnicott 1960) to indicate the condition under which most infants will thrive and reach most of their potential. The mother does not have to be perfect. For all but the most exceptionally fragile and demanding of children, she just has to be good enough. In fact, good enough fosters a better developmental environment than perfect, because the infant is required to fill in the blanks and develop personal resources when the mother is not perfectly attuned. According to this theory, the mothering ideal actually lies in that zone between perfect and not good enough.

Of course, we know this is true for our adult partner relationships as well. Perfection is a myth. The best of relationships are good enough—although some, obviously, are a little more good enough than others.

If you are reading this book, you're probably experiencing a lot of negatives in your relationship, so the question becomes: Do you feel positively about your partner and this relationship frequently enough to outweigh the obvious negatives? Are there enough good things to make the relationship still good enough?

Sometimes, the problem isn't how bad (intensity) the problems are, but how often they occur (frequency). Here are some questions to ask yourself that will help you assess the "good enough" factor.

EXERCISE:
Is There Enough Good Enough?

Think about the following questions and write your responses in your journal.

1. Has your relationship ever been good enough? Can you look back at times earlier on when you felt really positive about your partner and about the two of you together? If the answer is yes, then the odds of a better future are good. If the answer is no, then it is much less likely that you will be happier in the future.

2. Are you able to honestly say that you like him? Not every day or in every way, but in your fundamental values and ways of approaching your lives together. Do you still like touching each other, even if the "mojo" is not currently in place? If you truly like him but a lot of his current male-type depression behaviors are a problem, then the relationship has a fighting chance.

3. Is there one or more than one area of your life together that unites you and transcends the current wave of problems? For instance, religion? Raising kids together? Politics? Passion for the outdoors?

Most relationships can withstand crummy aspects and low periods as long as they share transcendent goals that help them rise above the distress. The transcendent shared goals and interest contribute to the likelihood of things being good enough.

Burnout: Duration

Sometimes there are no intense contract violations, but you just have a profound experience of exhaustion in this relationship. You still feel close to your partner, you feel compassion for what he has been going through, and you know that he is trying. And yet . . . In these situations, the problem isn't how bad (intensity) it is, nor how many times it keeps happening (frequency), but how long it lasts (duration) when it happens.

Love is not enough. You can still love your husband or boyfriend, yet decide that it is no longer the right thing for you two to be together. Love is necessary but not sufficient.

Most of you (just like most of the men you are involved with), for a thousand good reasons, can put up with problems and disappointments in a relationship and work to see it through. But you have to be able to see some light at the end of the tunnel. Even if your experience isn't unbearable and there are still plenty of positives in the relationship, you may feel irrevocably burned out because of how long the problems have been present and how far you see them extending into the future.

EXERCISE: Are You Burned Out?

Answer the following questions and write any accompanying thoughts in your journal.

1. Do you feel like you have given up trying to get some of the basic things that you need in the relationship, like communication, respect, and affection? Even though all of us learn to cope with fundamental disappointment in our relationship, some kinds of disappointments are more pervasive and more significant than others.

2. If you have been deeply hurt or betrayed in this relationship, is the pain slowly decreasing? Most of us can recover from pain in a relationship—as long as we see the train heading in the right direction. Are you progressively feeling closer and more trusting? If not, then the prospects for a positive future are bleak.

3. Ask yourself the question that author Mira Kirshenbaum (1996) asks in her excellent book, *Too Good to Leave, Too Bad to Stay*: If all the problems in your relationship were magically solved today, would you still feel ambivalent about whether to stay or leave?

POTENTIAL FOR CHANGE

When you approach your partner about what you need from him to help make the relationship good enough (and even better than good enough at some point), how does he take it?

The Man Who Doesn't Get It

Some men in this extremely meaningful conversation do not get what the hell you're talking about. They either cannot or simply refuse to see it. If the issues you're dealing with are significant enough, this kind of response can make it almost impossible for you to continue if you want at least a good-enough relationship. I don't mean that a defensive, rejecting reaction to the first time you broach an important issue is cause for divorce. But if your partner persistently avoids dealing with the problem after repeated attempts in every way that you can dream of, and after allowing him plenty of time and room to get used to the idea, you may be facing a dead end.

The Man Who Gets It but Doesn't Want to Change

Another man in this conversation may agree with you and acknowledge that something is wrong with him and his treatment of you. And then he may say that he is just not willing to change these things. For example, you tell him that the bad moods that overtake him lead him to treat the kids in a destructive, demeaning, and abusive fashion. And he may respond that he sees your point. But he may go on to tell you that he doesn't know how to change, and that he's unwilling to go into therapy, read books, go to parenting classes, consult with his pastor, take antidepressant medication, or do any of the other interventions that might make a meaningful difference. You can't wait for him to want to change forever.

One man whom I treated in couples therapy had been struggling for years with classic symptoms of male-type depression: restlessness, intermittent irritability and explosive temper, not revealing feelings other than criticisms, and frustration about ways in which his wife seemed controlling and unappreciative of him. He ended up having an affair. He realized that this was a problem that could easily destroy the marriage, but initially he refused to enter therapy with his wife, saying, "I'm not a 'therapy' kind of guy." He turned down suggestions about self-help books because he wasn't "a 'self-help book' kind of guy." When I suggested that he consider antidepressants, he said (you guessed it), "I'm just not an 'antidepressants' kind of guy." I responded, "I guess not. When things are going badly for you in your relationship, you have an affair. I guess you're an 'affair' kind of guy."

The Man Who Tries to Change but Can't

There is still one more kind of man with a different possible response here. This man acknowledges the problems. He is willing to change. He keeps trying. But he is consistently unsuccessful. If you really believe that your partner takes your concerns seriously and has the good intentions to try to offer you what you need but is stymied by the problem's complexity, then you're faced with a tough question. Your choice becomes a matter of what is good enough. Without the changes you're requesting, can the relationship be good enough to work for you? Almost all of you would answer in the negative if the behavior in question were repeated acts of violence or infidelity—the intensity is too high. Almost all of you would answer in the affirmative if the behavior in question were periodic episodes of sadness stemming from difficult events in his life that he talked about with you and didn't blame you for. And most of you would be somewhere in the middle if the problems were of medium intensity, medium frequency, and medium duration.

All you can do is to ask yourself these kinds of questions, weigh your needs and his, keep track of your values, accept some input from trusted others, and make your best call. I want relationships to work. I hope you all can find a way to stay. But for some of you this won't be the right path.

SUMMARY

Not every woman living with a depressed man has reached the point of extended unhappiness where she considers giving up on the relationship. For those who have, however, it's important to examine whether the disturbing behaviors have reached a level of intensity, frequency, or duration beyond what you can or should endure. It is also important to make your best possible determination about the potential for change. Even though a lot of things are not going well now, they may have been better in the past, and there may be a reasonable expectation that they will be better in the future. If so, the prospects for the relationship are good, or at least possible. If not, they are bleak, and the most self-respecting choice may be to leave.

AND, FINALLY . . .

Your mission is to show as much compassion as possible for what the depressed man in your life is going through—in all of the different ways this may be displayed. But you should also empower yourself to use whatever you can to help him, including setting limits when his behavior is not good for him or for you. The path with these complex issues can never be reduced to a simple formula, but the goal is always to do what is most likely to be best for him, for yourself, and for your relationship. I know you can do that.

Glossary of Terms

Broken mirror: The "mirroring" experience originates from the field of selfpsychology, where it is identified as the "mirroring selfobject." We rely on the response from another person to validate our sense of self. When we receive (or think we receive) a response that is negative, the mirror is broken and we feel depleted, empty, and depressed.

Depressiogenic: This identifies a behavior or condition that is likely to lead to depression, just like carcinogenic conditions are likely to lead to cancer. Usually used in describing thought patterns that generate or maintain depression.

Emotional intelligence: A modern measure of the capacity to identify feelings, express feelings, tolerate emotional distress, and experience empathy for others.

Emotional reasoning: From cognitive behavioral therapy, in which we make a false conclusion about the world based only on a current emotional state.

Good enough: A term originally coined in studies of mother-child interactions to indicate the condition under which most infants will thrive and reach most of their potential. The mother does not have to be perfect, just good enough. This also applies to adult relationships.

Imaginary crimes: Children often grow up believing that they have committed some emotional crime against their family or that they are at risk for doing so. The perception of having committed these crimes leads them to feel shame and often depression.

Male-type depression: In this pattern of male depression, men do not usually report sadness, but they do report feeling irritable or tremendously fatigued. They feel restless, agitated, and unsatisfiable. They act out rather than turning within. And they often become hostile and blaming.

Narcissistic injury: A term from self-psychology that describes a psychological blow to our sense of self or well-being.

Normative male alexithymia: The term describes mildly (or sometimes more severely) depressed men who struggle to identify and express their inner states.

Personal narrative: Any story or description that we generate to make sense of a life situation, including our relationships, personal history, or identity in the world. The word "narrative," by itself, is value-neutral: it may either be constructive or destructive, accurate or distorted.

Successive approximations: A procedure developed from learning theory that describes the pattern of progressively approaching a behavioral goal in baby steps.

Resources

UNDERSTANDING DEPRESSION

American Psychiatric Association. 2000. *Diagnostic and Statistical Manual of Mental Disorders DSM-IV-TR (Text Revision)*. Washington, D.C.: American Psychiatric Association.

Beck, A. 1988. *Love Is Never Enough*. New York: Harper & Row.

Burns, D. 1999. *The Feeling Good Handbook*. New York: Plume.

———. 1992. *Feeling Good: The New Mood Therapy*. New York: Avon Books.

Cousens, G. 2000. *Depression-Free for Life*. New York: HarperCollins.

Cronkite, K. 1994. *On the Edge of Darkness: Conversations about Conquering Depression*. New York: Delta Books.

Dowling, C. 1993. *You Mean I Don't Have to Feel This Way? New Help for Depression, Anxiety, and Addiction*. New York: Bantam Books.

Jamison, K. 1995. *An Unquiet Mind: A Memoir of Moods and Madness.* New York: Knopf.

McKay, M., and P. Fanning. 2000. *Self-Esteem.* Oakland, Calif.: New Harbinger Publications.

Seligman, M. 1998. *Learned Optimism: How to Change Your Mind and Your Life.* New York: Pocket Books.

Styron, W. 1990. *Darkness Visible: A Memoir of Madness.* New York: Random House.

Yapko, M. 1996. *Breaking the Patterns of Depression.* New York: Doubleday.

MALE DEPRESSION/MALE PSYCHOLOGY

Diamond, J. 1997. *Male Menopause.* Naperville, Ill.: Sourcebooks.

Goleman, D. 1995. *Emotional Intelligence.* New York: Bantam Books.

Hart, A. 2001. *Unmasking Male Depression.* Nashville, Tenn.: W Publishing.

Mandela, N. 1994. *Long Walk to Freedom: The Autobiography of Nelson Mandela.* London: Little Brown.

Pollack, W. 1998. *Real Boys.* New York: Henry Holt.

Real, T. 1997. *I Don't Want to Talk About It: Overcoming the Secret Legacy of Male Depression.* New York: Simon & Schuster.

Wexler, D. 2004. *When Good Men Behave Badly: Change Your Behavior, Change Your Relationship.* Oakland, Calif.: New Harbinger Publications.

Maledepression.com
http://www.maledepression.com
A "guy-friendly" site that offers support to and from men who suffer from depression and other mood disorders.

GENERAL RESOURCES ON DEPRESSION

World Wide Web Mental Health
http://www.mentalhealth.com/
Comprehensive, easy-to-use Web site. Excellent place to start for
a wide variety of information. Great section on medications, uses,
doses, side effects.

Depression FAQ (Frequently Asked Questions)
http://www.faqs.org/faqs/alt=support=depression/faq
Information on where to get help, books to read, a list of famous
people who suffer from depression, and Internet resources.

McMan's Depression and Bipolar Web
http://www.mcmanweb.com
User-friendly, easy-to-understand Web site with many links to
other resources. Greater focus on bipolar disorder but has testi-
monials from people who suffer from both illnesses. Links to latest
news and research in the area.

University of Michigan Depression Center
http://www.depressioncenter.org
Offers outstanding state-of-the-art education, treatment, and prevention strategies.

The Depression Center
http://www.depressioncenter.net
Web site with many links and resources about depression. For the
consumer and the clinician.

The Depression and Bipolar Support Alliance
http://www.dbsalliance.org
"Improving the lives of people living with mood disorders."
Friendly, easy to navigate. Uses simple, straightforward terminol-
ogy.

National Alliance for the Mentally Ill (NAMI)
http://www.nami.org
A support and advocacy organization of consumers, families, and
friends of people with severe mental illness with over 1,200 state
and local affiliates. Excellent section on finding support.

National Institute of Mental Health (NIMH)
http://menanddepression.nimh.nih.gov/
"Real Men, Real Depression" campaign offers an informative, free brochure, "Men and Depression." Send e-mail to menanddepression@mail.nih.gov or call toll-free (866) 227-6464.

Depression Awareness, Recognition, and Treatment (D/ART):
http://www.brooklane.org/whitepgs/depression/geninfo.html
D/ART is a professional and public education program sponsored by NIMH in collaboration with private organizations and citizens.

National Mental Health Association
http://www.nmha.org
Informative, easy-to-use Web site with a "therapist finder" sponsored by *Psychology Today* that finds therapists in your area, offering the name, contact information, and a personal statement by the therapist.

MDAdvice.COM
http://www.mdadvice.com/topics/depression/info
User-friendly Web site that provides a variety of information and resources on depression and many other medical issues. Offers bulletin boards and live chat on depression.

Christian LifeSkills
http://www.christianlifeskills.com
A Christian-based resource for healthy life skills and mental-health resources from a Christian orientation.

Mental Help Net
http://www.mentalhelp.net/
Designed and maintained by clinical psychologists, this site is dedicated to educating the public about mental health, wellness, and family and relationship issues and concerns.

TRAUMA ISSUES

Engel, L., and T. Ferguson. 1990. *Imaginary Crimes*. Boston: Houghton Mifflin.

Herman, J. L. 1992. *Trauma and Recovery*. New York: Basic Books.

COPING WITH A PARTNER'S DEPRESSION

Adamec, C. 1996. *How to Live with a Mentally Ill Person.* New York: John Wiley & Sons.

Al-Anon Family Group Headquarters. 1981. *Detachment.* Virginia Beach, Virg.: Al-Anon Family Group Headquarters.

Carter, R., with S. K. Golant. 1996. *Helping Yourself Help Others: A Book for Caregivers.* New York: Times Books.

Fast, J., and J. Preston. 2004. *Loving Someone with Bipolar Disorder.* Oakland, Calif.: New Harbinger Publications.

Golant, M., and S. Golant. 1997. *What to Do When Someone You Love Is Depressed.* New York: Henry Holt.

Kirshenbaum, M. 1996. *Too Good to Leave, Too Bad to Stay.* New York: Penguin Books.

Oster, G., and S. Montgomery. 1995. *Helping Your Depressed Teenager: A Guide for Parents and Caregivers.* New York: John Wiley & Sons.

Podell, R., with P. Shimer. 1992. *Contagious Emotions: Staying Well When Your Loved One Is Depressed.* New York: Pocket Books.

ANTIDEPRESSANT MEDICATION

Kramer, P. 1993. *Listening to Prozac.* New York: Viking Penguin.

Stahl, S. 2000. *Essential Psychopharmacology.* Cambridge, UK: Cambridge University Press.

PharmWeb
http://www.pharmweb.net
The Internet drug index. Look up information on any drug.

Prozac.com
http://www.prozac.com
Everything you wanted to know about Prozac and more.

VISUALIZATION AND RELAXATION

Benson, H. 1975. *The Relaxation Response.* New York: Avon Books.

Gawain, S. 1995. *Creative Visualization.* New York: Bantam Books.

Kabat-Zinn, J. 1990. *Full Catastrophe Living.* New York: Delta.

Samuels, M. 1975. *Seeing with the Mind's Eye.* New York: Random House.

ALTERNATIVE/LIFESTYLE INTERVENTIONS

Fredrickson, B. L. 2000. Cultivating positive emotions to optimize health and well-being. *Prevention and Treatment* 3, article 0001a (March 7), http://www.journals.apa.org/prevention/volume3/pre0030001a.html.

Somer, E. 1995. *Food and Mood: The Complete Guide to Eating Well and Feeling Your Best.* New York: Henry Holt.

HedWeb: Good Drug Guide
http://www.biopsychiatry.com
Wordy and not easy on the eye, nevertheless, this Web site provides down-to-earth information on the impact of legal and illegal drugs on our mood and offers healthy alternatives. Definitely worth a look for those seeking alternative approaches.

NutritionalSupplements.com
http://www.nutritionalsupplements.com
Nutritional resources for depression.

INFIDELITY

Pittman, F. 1990. *Private Lies: Infidelity and Betrayal of Intimacy.* New York: W. W. Norton.

Spring, J. 1996. *After the Affair: Healing the Pain and Rebuilding Trust When a Partner Has Been Unfaithful.* New York: HarperCollins.

WHERE TO GET HELP

If you are unsure where to go for help, check the Yellow Pages under "mental health," "health," "social services," "suicide prevention," "crisis intervention services," "hotlines," "hospitals," or "physicians" for phone numbers and addresses. In times of crisis, the emergency room doctor at a hospital may be able to provide temporary help for an emotional problem and will be able to tell you where and how to get further help.

Listed below are the types of people and places that will make a referral or be able to provide diagnostic and treatment services.

- Family doctors
- Mental-health specialists such as psychiatrists, psychologists, social workers, or mental-health counselors
- Health maintenance organizations (HMOs)
- Community mental-health centers
- Hospital psychiatry departments and outpatient clinics
- State hospital outpatient clinics
- Family-service agencies, social agencies, or clergy
- Private clinics and facilities
- Employee-assistance programs
- Local medical and/or psychiatric or psychology societies

References

American Association of Marriage and Family Therapists. Intimacy and Depression: The Silent Epidemic. http://www.aamft.org/families/intimacy_depression/antidepressants.htm. (accessed 2004).

American Psychiatric Association. 2000. *Diagnostic and Statistical Manual of Mental Disorders DSM-IV-TR (Text Revision)*. Washington, D.C.: American Psychiatric Association.

Azar, B. 2000. A new stress paradigm for women. *Monitor on Psychology*, 31(7):42–43.

Bandura, A. 1997. *Self-Efficacy: The Exercise of Control*. New York: Freeman.

Beck, A. 1976. *Cognitive Therapy and the Emotional Disorders*. New York: Harper & Row.

Brown, G., and T. Harris. 1978. *Social Origins of Depression*. London: Tavistock.

Burns, D. 1999. *The Feeling Good Handbook*. New York: Plume.

Colarusso, C., and R. Nemiroff. 1981. *Adult Development*. New York: Plenum Press.

Diamond, J. 1997. *Male Menopause*. Naperville, Ill.: Sourcebooks.

Engel, L., and T. Ferguson. 1990. *Imaginary Crimes*. Boston: Houghton Mifflin.

Foreman, J. Health Sense. Roots of violence may lie in damaged brain cells. *Los Angeles Times*. April 29, 2002.

Gottman, J. 1999. *The Marriage Clinic*. New York: W. W. Norton.

Hales, D., and R. Hales. 2004. Too tough to seek help? *Parade Magazine*, June 20.

Jung, C. 1977. *C. G. Jung Speaking*. Edited by William McGuire and R. F. C. Hull. Princeton, N.J.: Princeton University Press.

Kabat-Zinn, J. 1990. *Full Catastrophe Living*. New York: Delta.

Kirshenbaum, M. 1996. *Too Good to Leave, Too Bad to Stay*. New York: Penguin Books.

Levant, R. 1998. Desperately seeking language: Understanding, assessing, and treating normative male alexithymia. In *New Psychotherapy for Men*, ed. W. Pollack and R. Levant. New York: John Wiley & Sons.

Linehan, M. 1993. *Skills Training Manual for Treating Borderline Personality Disorder*. New York: Guilford Press.

Mandela, N. 1994. *Long Walk to Freedom: The Autobiography of Nelson Mandela*. London: Little Brown.

McKay, M., and P. Fanning. 2000. *Self-Esteem*. Oakland, Calif.: New Harbinger Publications.

National Institute of Mental Health. 2000. Depression. http://www.nimh.nih.gov/publicat/depression.cfm.

———. 2002. Medications. http://www.nimh.nih.gov/publicat/medicate.cfm.

———. Real Men, Real Depression. http://menanddepression.nimh.nih.gov (accessed 2004).

Nolen-Hoeksema, S. 1993. Sex differences in control of depression. In *Handbook of Mental Control*, ed. D. Wegner and J. Pennebaker, 239–257. Englewood Cliffs, N.J.: Prentice Hall.

Phillips, R., and J. Slaughter. 2000. Depression and sexual desire. *American Family Physician*, August 15.

Pollack, W. 1998a. Mourning, melancholia, and masculinity: Recognizing and treating depression in men. In *New Psychotherapy for Men*, ed. W. Pollack and R. Levant. New York: John Wiley & Sons.

———. 1998b. *Real Boys*. New York: Henry Holt.

Potts, M., M. Burnam, and K. Wells. 1991. Gender differences in depressive detection: A comparison of clinician diagnosis and standardized assessment. *Psychological Assessment* 3(4):609–665.

Real, T. 1997. *I Don't Want to Talk About It: Overcoming the Secret Legacy of Male Depression*. New York: Fireside.

Seligman, M. 1998. *Learned Optimism*. New York: Pocket Books.

———. Positive Psychology, Positive Prevention, and Positive Therapy. http://www.positivepsychology.org/ppsnyderchapter.htm. (accessed 2004).

Servan-Schreiber, D. 2004. Run for your life. *Psychotherapy Networker*, July/August, 47–67.

Shapiro, S. 1995. *Talking with Patients: A Self-Psychological View*. New York: Jason Aronson.

Tice, D., and R. Baumeister. 1993. Controlling anger: Self-induced emotion change, in *Handbook of Mental Control*, ed. D. Wegner and J. Pennebaker. Englewood Cliffs, N.J.: Prentice Hall.

University of Michigan Depression Center. www.depressioncenter.org (accessed 2005).

Viorst, J. 1986. *Necessary Losses*. New York: Simon & Schuster.

Weiss, J., and H. Sampson. 1986. *The Psychoanalytic Process*. New York: Guilford Press.

Wenzlaff, R. 1993. The mental control of depression, in *Handbook of Mental Control*, ed. D. Wegner and J. Pennebaker, (239–257). Englewood Cliffs, N.J.: Prentice Hall.

Wexler, D. 2004. *When Good Men Behave Badly: Change Your Behavior, Change Your Relationship*. Oakland, Calif.: New Harbinger Publications.

WholeHealthMD. Omega-3 Fatty Acids. http://www.wholehealthmd.com/refshelf/substances_view/1,1525,992,00.html (accessed 2005).

Winnicott, D. 1960. The theory of the parent-child relationship. *International Journal of Psychoanalysis* 41:585–595.

Yapko, M. 1996. *Breaking the Patterns of Depression*. New York: Doubleday.

Zajecka J., S. Mitchell, and J. Fawcett. 1997. Treatment-emergent changes in sexual function with selective serotonin reuptake inhibitors as measured with the Rush Sexual Inventory. *Psychopharmacology Bulletin* 33:755–760.

Zillman, D. 1993. Mental control of angry aggression, in *Handbook of Mental Control*, ed. D. Wegner and J. Pennebaker. Englewood Cliffs, N.J.: Prentice Hall.

David B. Wexler, Ph.D., is a clinical psychologist in San Diego specializing in the treatment of relationships in conflict and the executive director of the Relationship Training Institute. He has trained professionals internationally on his pioneering ideas for relationship development and the prevention and treatment of domestic violence. Wexler is the author of *When Good Men Behave Badly,* and he has been featured on *The Dr. Phil Show* and *The Today Show;* in the *Washington Post, O Magazine, Cosmopolitan, Redbook,* and *Men's Health;* and on dozens of radio and TV programs throughout North America. His work helps to educate the public about relationships in conflict and conflict-resolutions strategies.

Foreword writer **Terrence Real,** best-selling author of *I Don't Want to Talk About It: Overcoming the Secret Legacy of Male Depression* and *How Can I Get Through to You? Reconnecting Men and Women,* is a senior faculty member of the Family Institute of Cambridge in Cambridge, MA, and director of the Gender Relations Program at the Meadows Institute in Arizona.

Some Other
New Harbinger Titles

Depressed and Anxious, Item 3635 $19.95

Angry All the Time, Item 3929 $13.95

Handbook of Clinical Psychopharmacology for Therapists, 4th edition, Item 3996 $55.95

Writing For Emotional Balance, Item 3821 $14.95

Surviving Your Borderline Parent, Item 3287 $14.95

When Anger Hurts, 2nd edition, Item 3449 $16.95

Calming Your Anxious Mind, Item 3384 $12.95

Ending the Depression Cycle, Item 3333 $17.95

Your Surviving Spirit, Item 3570 $18.95

Coping with Anxiety, Item 3201 $10.95

The Agoraphobia Workbook, Item 3236 $19.95

Loving the Self-Absorbed, Item 3546 $14.95

Transforming Anger, Item 352X $10.95

Don't Let Your Emotions Run Your Life, Item 3090 $17.95

Why Can't I Ever Be Good Enough, Item 3147 $13.95

Your Depression Map, Item 3007 $19.95

Successful Problem Solving, Item 3023 $17.95

Working with the Self-Absorbed, Item 2922 $14.95

The Procrastination Workbook, Item 2957 $17.95

Coping with Uncertainty, Item 2965 $11.95

The BDD Workbook, Item 2930 $18.95

You, Your Relationship, and Your ADD, Item 299X $17.95

The Stop Walking on Eggshells Workbook, Item 2760 $18.95

Conquer Your Critical Inner Voice, Item 2876 $15.95

The PTSD Workbook, Item 2825 $17.95

Hypnotize Yourself Out of Pain Now!, Item 2809 $14.95

Call **toll free, 1-800-748-6273,** or log on to our online bookstore at **www.newharbinger.com** to order. Have your Visa or Mastercard number ready. Or send a check for the titles you want to New Harbinger Publications, Inc., 5674 Shattuck Ave., Oakland, CA 94609. Include $4.50 for the first book and 75¢ for each additional book, to cover shipping and handling. (California residents please include appropriate sales tax.) Allow two to five weeks for delivery.

Prices subject to change without notice.